Slavery Ordained of God

By Rev. Fred. A. Ross

SLAVERY ORDAINED OF GOD

By

Rev. Fred. A. Ross, D.D.

"The powers that be are ordained of God." Romans xiii. 1.

TO The Men NORTH AND SOUTH, WHO HONOR THE WORD OF GOD AND LOVE THEIR COUNTRY.

Preface.

The book I give to the public, is not made up of isolated articles. It is one harmonious demonstration--that slavery is part of the government ordained in certain conditions of fallen mankind. I present the subject in the form of speeches, actually delivered, and letters written just as published. I adopt this method to make a readable book.

I give it to the North and South--to maintain harmony among Christians, and to secure the integrity of the union of this great people.

This harmony and union can be preserved only by the view presented in this volume,--_i.e._ that _slavery is of God_, and to continue for the good of the slave, the good of the master, the good of the whole American family, until another and better destiny may be unfolded.

The _one great idea_, which I submit to North and South, is expressed in the speech, first in order, delivered in the General Assembly of the Presbyterian Church, Buffalo, May 27, 1853. I therein say:-

"Let us then, North and South, bring our minds to comprehend _two ideas_, and submit to their irresistible power. Let the Northern philanthropist learn from the Bible that the relation of master and slave is not sin per se. Let him learn that God says nowhere it is sin. Let him learn that sin is the transgression of the law; and where there is no law there is no sin, and that the Golden Rule may exist in the relations of slavery. Let him learn that slavery is simply an evil in certain circumstances. Let him learn that equality is only the highest form of social life; that subjection to authority, even _slavery_, may, in _given conditions_, be for a time better than freedom to the slave of any complexion. Let him learn that _slavery_, like _all evils_, has its corresponding and _greater good_; that the Southern slave, though degraded _compared with his master, is elevated and ennobled compared with his brethren in Africa_. Let the Northern man learn these things, and be wise to cultivate the spirit that will harmonize with his brethren of the South, who are lovers of liberty as truly as himself: And let the Southern Christian-- nay, the Southern man of every grade--comprehend that God never intended the relation of master and slave to be perpetual. Let him give up the theory of Voltaire, that the negro is of a different species. Let him yield the semi-infidelity of Agassiz, that God created different races of the same species--in swarms, like bees--for Asia, Europe, America, Africa, and the islands of the sea. Let him believe that slavery, although not a sin, is a degraded condition,-- the evil, the curse on the South,--yet having blessings in its time to the South and to the Union. Let him know that slavery is to pass away in the fulness of Providence. Let the South believe this, and prepare to obey the hand that moves their destiny."

All which comes after, in the speech delivered in New York, 1856, and in the letters, is just the expansion of this one controlling thought, which must be understood, believed, and acted out North and South.

The Author.

Written in Cleveland, Ohio, May 28, 1857.

Contents.

Speech Before the General Assembly at Buffalo Speech Before the General

Assembly at New York Letter to Rev. A. Blackburn What Is the Foundation of Moral Obligation?

Letters to Rev. A. Barnes:--

I.--Results of the slavery agitation--Declaration of Independence-- The way men are made infidels--Testimonies of General Assemblies II.--Government over man a divine institute III.--Man-stealing IV.--The Golden Rule

Speech Delivered at Buffalo, Before the General Assembly of the Presbyterian Church.

To understand the following speech, the reader will be pleased to learn--if he don't know already--that the General Assembly of the Presbyterian Church, before its division in 1838, and since,--both Old School and New School,--has been, for forty years and more, bearing testimony, after a fashion, against the system of slavery; that is to say, affirming, in one breath, that slave-holding is a "blot on our holy religion," &c. &c.; and then, in the next utterance, making all sorts of apologies and justifications for the slave-holder. Thus: this august body has been in the habit of telling the Southern master (especially in the Detroit resolutions of 1850) that he is a _sinner_, hardly meet to be called a _Christian_; but, nevertheless, if he will only sin "from unavoidable necessity, imposed by the laws of the States,"--if he will only sin under the "obligations of guardianship,"--if he will only sin "from the demands of humanity,"--why, then, forsooth, he may be a slave-holder as long as he has a mind to. Yea, he may hold one slave, one hundred or one thousand slaves, and till the day of judgment.

Happening to be in attendance, as a member of the body, in Buffalo, May, 1853, when, as usual, the system of slavery was touched, in a series of questions sent down to the church courts below, I made the following remarks, in good-natured ridicule of such preposterous and stultifying testimony; and, as an argument, opening the views I have since reproduced in the second speech of this volume, delivered in the General Assembly which convened in New York, May, 1856, and also in the letters following:--

BUFFALO, FRIDAY, May 27, 1853.

The order of the day was reached at a quarter before eleven, and the report read again,--viz.:

"1. That this body shall reaffirm the doctrine of the second resolution adopted by the General Assembly, convened in Detroit, in 1850, and,

"2. That with an express disavowal of any intention to be impertinently inquisitorial, and for the sole purpose of arriving at the truth, so as to correct misapprehensions and allay all causeless irritation, a committee be appointed of one from each of the synods of Kentucky, Tennessee, Missouri, and Virginia, who shall be requested to report to the next General Assembly on the following points:--1. The number of slave-holders in connection with the churches, and the number of slaves held by them. 2. The extent to which slaves are held from an unavoidable necessity imposed by the laws of the States, the obligations of guardianship, and the demands of humanity. 3. Whether the Southern churches regard the sacredness of the marriage relation as it exists among the slaves; whether baptism is duly administered to the children of the slaves professing Christianity, and in general, to what extent and in what manner provision is made for the religious well-being of the slave," &c. &c.

Dr. Ross moved to amend the report by substituting the following,--with an express disavowal of being impertinently inquisitorial:--that a committee of one from each of the Northern synods of ---- be appointed, who shall be requested to report to the next General Assembly,--

1. The number of Northern church-members concerned, directly or indirectly, in building and fitting out ships for the African slave-trade, and the slave-trade between the States.

2. The number of Northern church-members who traffic with slave-holders, and are seeking to make money by selling them negro-clothing, handcuffs, and cowhides.

3. The number of Northern church-members who have sent orders to New Orleans, and other Southern cities, to have slaves sold, to pay debts owing them from the South. [See Uncle Tom's Cabin.]

4. The number of Northern church-members who buy the cotton, sugar, rice, tobacco, oranges, pine-apples, figs, ginger, cocoa, melons, and a thousand other things, raised by slave-labor.

5. The number of Northern church-members who have intermarried with slave-holders, and have thus become slave-owners themselves, or enjoy the wealth made by the blood of the slave,--especially if there be any Northern ministers of the gospel in such a predicament.

6. The number of Northern church-members who are the descendants of the men who kidnapped negroes in Africa and brought them to Virginia and New England in former years.

7. The aggregate and individual wealth of members thus descended, and what action is best to compel them to disgorge this blood-stained gold, or to compel them to give dollar for dollar in equalizing the loss of the South by emancipation.

8. The number of Northern church-members, ministers especially, who have advocated murder in resistance to the laws of the land.

9. The number of Northern church-members who own stock in under-ground railroads, running off fugitive slaves, and in Sabbath-breaking railroads and canals.

10. That a special commission be sent up Red River, to ascertain whether

Legree, who whipped Uncle Tom to death, (and who was a Northern _gentleman_,) be not still in connection with some Northern church in good and regular standing.

11. The number of Northern church-members who attend meetings of Spiritual Rappers,--or Bloomers,--or Women's-Rights Conventions.

12. The number of Northern church-members who are cruel husbands.

13. The number of Northern church-members who are hen-pecked husbands.

[As it is always difficult to know the temper of speaker and audience from a printed report, it is due alike to Dr. R., to the whole Assembly, and the galleries, to say, that he, in reading these resolutions, and throughout his speech, evinced great good-humour and kindness of feeling, which was equally manifested by the Assembly and spectators, repeatedly, while he was on the floor.]

Dr. Ross then proceeded:--Mr. Moderator, I move this amendment in the best spirit. I desire to imitate the committee in their refinement and delicacy of distinction. I disavow all intention to be impertinently inquisitorial. I intend to be inquisitorial, as the committee say they are,--but not impertinently so. No, sir; not at all; not at all. (Laughter.) Well, sir, we of the South, who desire the removal of the evil of slavery, and believe it will pass away in the developments of Providence, are grieved when we read your graphic, shuddering pictures of the "middle passage,"--the slave-ship, piling up her canvas, as the shot pours after her from English or American guns,--see her again and again hurrying hogshead after hogshead, filled with living slaves, into the deep, and, thus lightened, escape. Sir, what horror to believe that clipper-ship was built by the hands of Northern, noisy Abolition church-members! ["Yes, I know some in New York and Boston," said one in the crowd.] Again, sir, when we walk along your _Broadways_, and see, as we do, the soft hands of your church-members sending off to the South, not only clothing for the slave, but manacles and whips, manufactured expressly for him,--what must we think of your consistency of character? [True, true.] And what must we think of your self-righteousness, when we know your church-members order the sale of slaves,--yes, slaves such as St. Clair's,--and under circumstances involving all the separations and all the loathsome things you so mournfully deplore? Your Mrs. Stowe says so, and it is so, without her testimony. I have read that splendid, bad book. Splendid in its genius, over which I have wept, and laughed, and got mad, (here some one said, "All at the same time?") yes--all at the same time. Bad in its theology, bad in its morality, bad in its temporary evil influence here in the North, in England, and on the continent of Europe; bad, because her isolated cruelties will be taken (whether so meant by her or not) as the general condition of Southern life,--while her Shelbys, and St. Clairs, and Evas, will be looked upon as angel-visitors, lingering for a moment in that earthly hell. The impression made by the book is a falsehood.

  Sir, why do your Northern church-members and philanthropists buy Southern products at all? You know you are purchasing cotton, rice, sugar, sprinkled with blood, literally, you say, from the lash of the driver! Why do you buy? What's the difference between my filching this blood-stained cotton from the outraged negro, and your standing by, taking it from me? What's the difference? You, yourselves, say, in your abstractions, there is no difference; and yet you daily stain your hands in this horrid traffic. You hate the traitor, but you love the treason. Your ladies, too,--oh, how they shun the slave-owner _at a distance_, in _the abstract_! But alas, when they see him in the _concrete_,--when they see the slave-owner _himself_, standing before them,--not the brutal driver, but the splendid gentleman, with his unmistakable grace of carriage and ease of manners,--why, lo, behold the lady says, "Oh, fie on your slavery!--what a wretch you are! But, indeed, sir, I love your sugar,--and truly, truly, sir, wretch as you are, I love you too." Your gentlemen talk just the same way when they behold our matchless women. And well for us all it is, that your good taste, and hearts, can thus appreciate our genius, and accomplishments, and fascinations, and loveliness, and sugar, and cotton. Why, sir, I heard this morning, from one pastor only, of two or three of his members thus intermarried in the South. May I thus give the mildest rebuke to your inconsistency of conduct? (Much good-natured excitement.)

Sir, may we know who are the descendants of the New England kidnappers? What is their wealth? Why, here you are, all around me. You, gentlemen, made the best of that bargain. And you have kept every dollar of your money from the charity of emancipating the slave. You have left us, unaided, to give millions. Will you now come to our help? Will you give dollar for dollar to equalize our loss? [Here many voices cried out, "Yes, yes, we will."]

Yes, yes? Then pour out your millions. Good. I may thank you personally. My own emancipated slaves would to-day be worth greatly more than $20,000. Will you give me back $10,000? Good. I need it now.

I recommend to you, sirs, to find out your advocates of _murder_,--your owners of stock in under-ground railroads,--your Sabbath-breakers for money. I particularly urge you to find Legree, who whipped Uncle Tom to death. He is a Northern _gentleman_, although having a somewhat Southern name. Now, sir, you know the Assembly was embarrassed all yesterday by the inquiry how the Northern churches may find their absent members, and what to do with them. Here then, sir, is a chance for you. Send a committee up Red River. You may find Legree to be a Garrison, Phillips, Smith, or runaway husband from some Abby Kelly. [Here Rev. Mr. Smith protested against Legree being proved to be a Smith. Great laughter. [Footnote: This gentleman was soon after made a D.D., and I think in part for that witticism.]] I move that you bring him back to lecture on the cuteness there is in leaving a Northern church, going South, changing his name, buying slaves, and calculating, without _guessing_, what the profit is of killing a negro with inhuman labor above the gain of treating him with kindness.

I have little to say of spirit-rappers, women's-rights conventionists, Bloomers, cruel husbands, or hen-pecked. But, if we may believe your own serious as well as caricature writers, you have things up here of which we down South know very little indeed. Sir, we have no young Bloomers, with hat to one side, cigar in mouth, and cane tapping the boot, striding up to a mincing young gentleman with long curls, attenuated waist, and soft velvet face,--the boy-lady to say, "May I see you home, sir?" and the lady-boy to reply, "I thank ye--no; pa will send the carriage." Sir, we of the South don't understand your women's-rights conventions. Women have their wrongs. "The Song of the Shirt,"--Charlotte Elizabeth,--many, many laws,--tell her wrongs. But your convention ladies despise the Bible. Yes, sir; and we of the South are afraid _of them_, and for you. When women despise the Bible, what next? _Paris,--then the City of the Great Salt Lake,--then Sodom, before_ and after the Dead Sea. Oh, sir, if slavery tends in any way to give the honour of chivalry to Southern young gentlemen towards ladies, and the exquisite delicacy and heavenly integrity and love to Southern maid and matron, it has then a glorious blessing with its curse.

Sir, your inquisitorial committee, and the North so far as represented by them, (a small fraction, I know,) have, I take it, caught a Tartar this time. Boys say with us, and everywhere, I _reckon_, "You worry my dog, and I'll worry your cat." Sir, it is just simply a _fixed fact: the South will not submit to these questions_. No, not for an instant. We will not permit you to approach us at all. If we are morbidly sensitive, you have made us so. But you are directly and grossly violating the Constitution of the Presbyterian Church. The book forbids you to put such questions; the book forbids _you to begin discipline_; the book forbids your sending this committee to help common fame bear testimony against us; the book guards the honour of our humblest member, minister, church, presbytery, against all this impertinently-inquisitorial action. Have you a _prosecutor_, with his definite charge and witnesses? Have you _Common Fame_, with her specified charges and witnesses? Have you a request from the South that you send a committee to inquire into slanders? No. Then hands off. As gentlemen you may ask us these questions,--we will answer you. But, ecclesiastically, you cannot speak in this matter. You have no power to move as you propose.

I beg leave to say, just here, that Tennessee [Footnote: At that time I resided in Tennessee.] will be more calm under this movement than any other slave-region. Tennessee has been ever high above the storm, North and South,--especially we of the mountains. Tennessee!--"there she is,--look at her,"--binding this Union together like a great, long, broad, deep stone,--more splendid than all in the temple of Baalbec or Solomon. Tennessee!--there she is, in her calm valour. I will not lower her by calling her unconquerable, for she has never been assailed; but I call her ever-victorious. King's Mountain,--her pioneer battles:--Talladega, Emucfau, Horse-shoe, New Orleans, San Jacinto, Monterey, the Valley of Mexico. Jackson represented her well in his chivalry from South Carolina,--his fiery courage from Virginia and Kentucky,--all tempered by Scotch-Irish Presbyterian prudence from Tennessee. We, in his spirit, have looked on this storm for years untroubled. Yes, Jackson's old bones rattled in their grave when that infamous disunion convention met in Nashville, and its members turned pale and fled aghast. Yes, Tennessee, in her mighty million, feels secure; and, in her perfect preparation to discuss this question, politically, ecclesiastically, morally, metaphysically, or physically, with the extreme North or South, she is willing and able to persuade others to be calm. In this connection, I wish to say, for the South to the North, and to the world, that we have no fears from our slave-population. There might be a momentary insurrection and bloodshed; but destruction to the black man would be inevitable. The Greeks and Romans controlled immense masses of white slaves,--many of them as intelligent as their lords. Schoolmasters, fabulists, and poets were slaves. Athens, with her thirty thousand freemen, governed half a million of bondmen. Single Roman patricians owned thirty thousand. If, then, the phalanx and the legion mastered such slaves for ages, when battle was physical force of man to man, how certain it is that infantry, cavalry, and artillery could hold in bondage millions of Africans for a thousand years!

But, dear brethren, our Southern philanthropists do not seek to have this unending bondage; Oh, no, no. And I earnestly entreat you to "stand still and see the salvation of the Lord." Assume a masterly inactivity, and you will behold all you desire and pray for,--you will see America liberated from the curse of slavery.

The great question of the world is, WHAT IS TO BE THE FUTURE OF THE AMERICAN SLAVE?--WHAT IS TO BE THE FUTURE OF THE AMERICAN MASTER? The following _extract from the "Charleston Mercury"_ gives my view of the subject with great and condensed particularity:--

"Married, Thursday, 26th inst., the Hon. Cushing Kewang, Secretary of State of the United States, to Laura, daughter of Paul Coligny, Vice-President of the United States, and one of our noblest Huguenot families. We learn that this distinguished gentleman, with his bride, will visit his father, the Emperor of China, at his summer palace, in Tartary, north of Pekin, and return to the Vice-President's Tea Pavilion, on Cooper River, ere the meeting of Congress." The editor of the "Mercury" goes on to say: "This marriage in high life is only one of many which have signalized that immense emigration from Christianized China during the last seventy-five years, whereby Charleston has a population of 1,250,000, and the State of South Carolina over 5,000,000,--an emigration which has wonderfully harmonized with the great exodus of the negro race to Africa." [Some gentleman here requested to know of Dr. Ross the date of the "Charleston Mercury" recording this marriage. The doctor replied, "The date is 27th May, 1953, exactly one hundred years from this day." Great laughter.]

Sir, this is a dream; but it is not all a dream. No, I verily believe you have there the Gordian knot of slavery untied; you have there the solution of the problem; you have there the curtain up, and the last scene in the last act of the great drama of Ham.

I am satisfied with the tendencies of things. I stand on the mountain-peak above the clouds. I see, far beyond the storm, the calm sea and blue sky; I see the Canaan of the African. I like to stand there on the Nebo of his exodus, and look across, not the Jordan, but the Atlantic. I see the African crossing as certainly as if I gazed upon the ocean divided by a great wind, and piled up in walls of green glittering glass on either hand, the dry ground, the marching host, and the pillar of cloud and of fire. I look over upon the Niger, black with death to the white man, instinct with life to the children of Ham. There is the black man's home. Oh, how strange that you of the North see not how you degrade him when you keep him here! You will not let him vote; you will not let him rise to honors or social equality; you will not let him hold a pew in your churches. Send him away, then; tell him, begone. Be urgent, like the Egyptians: send him out of this land. _There_, in his fatherland, he will exhibit his own type of Christianity. He is, of all races, the most gentle and kind. The _man_, the most submissive; the _woman_, the most affectionate. What other slaves would love their masters better than themselves?--rock them and fan them in their cradles? caress them--how tenderly!--boys and girls? honor them, grown up, as superior beings? and, in thousands of illustrious instances, be willing to give life, and, in fact, die, to serve or save them? Verily, verily, this emancipated race may reveal the most amiable form of spiritual life, and the jewel may glitter on the Ethiop's brow in meaning more sublime than all in the poet's imagery. Brethren, let them go; and, when they are gone,--ay, before they go away,--rear a monument; let it grow in greatness, if not on your highest mountain, in your hearts,--in lasting memory of the South,--in memory of your wrong to the South,--in memory of the self-denial of the South, and her philanthropy in training the slave to be free, enlightened, and Christian.

Can all this be? Can this double emigration civilize Africa and more than re-people the South? Yes; and I regard the difficulties presented here, in Congress, or the country, as little worth. God intends both emigrations. And, without miracle, he will accomplish both. Difficulties! There are no difficulties. Half a million emigrate to our shores, from Ireland, and all Europe, every year. And you gravely talk of difficulties in the negro's way to Africa! Verily, God will unfold their destiny as fast, and as fully, as he sees best for the highest good of the slave, the highest good of the master, and the glory of Christ in Africa.

And, sir, there are forty thousand Chinese in California. And in Cuba, this day, American gentlemen are cultivating sugar, with Chinese hired labor, more profitably than the Spaniards and their slaves. Oh! there is China--half the population of the globe--just fronting us across that peaceful sea,--her poor, living on rats and a pittance of red rice,--her rich, hoarding millions in senseless idolatry, or indulging in the luxuries of birds'-nests and roasted ice. Massed together, they must migrate. Where can they go? They must come to our shores. They must come, even did God forbid them. But he will hasten their coming. They can live in the extremest South. It is their latitude,--their side of the ocean. They can cultivate cotton, rice, sugar, tea, and the silkworm. Their skill, their manipulation, is unrivalled. Their commonest gong you can neither make nor explain. They are a law-abiding people, without castes, accustomed to rise by merit to highest distinctions, and capable of the noblest training, when their idolatry, which is waxing old as a garment, shall be folded up as a vesture and changed for that whose years shall not fail. The English ambassador assures us that the Chinese negotiator of the late treaty was a splendid gentleman, and a diplomatist to move in any court of Europe. Shem, then, can mingle with Japheth in America.

The Chinese must come. God will bring them. He will fulfil Benton's noble thought. The railroad must complete the voyage of Columbus. The statue of the Genoese, on some peak of the Rocky Mountains, high above the flying cars, must point to the West, saying, "There is the East! There is India and Cathay."

Let us, then, North and South, bring our minds to comprehend _two ideas_, and submit to their irresistible power. Let the Northern philanthropist learn from the Bible that the relation of master and slave is not sin per se. Let him learn that God nowhere says it is sin. Let him learn that sin is the transgression of the law; and where there is no law, there is no sin; and that the golden rule may exist in the relations of slavery. Let him learn that slavery is simply an evil in certain circumstances. Let him learn that equality is only the highest form of social life; that subjection to authority, even _slavery_, may, in _given conditions_, be for a time better than freedom to the slave, of any complexion. Let him learn that _slavery_, like _all evils_, has its corresponding and _greater good_; that the Southern slave, though degraded _compared with his master_, is elevated and ennobled compared with his brethren in Africa. Let the Northern man learn these things, and be wise to cultivate the spirit that will harmonize with his brethren of the South, who are lovers of liberty as truly as himself. And let the Southern Christian--nay, the Southern man of every grade--comprehend that God never intended the relation of master and slave to be perpetual. Let him give up the theory of Voltaire, that the negro is of a different species. Let him yield the semi-infidelity of Agassiz, that God created different races of the same species--in swarms, like bees--for Asia, Europe, America, Africa, and the islands of the sea. Let him believe that slavery, although not a sin, is a degraded condition,--the evil, the curse on the South,--yet having blessings in its time to the South and to the Union. Let him know that slavery is to pass away, in the fulness of Providence. Let the South believe this, and prepare to obey the hand that moves their destiny.

Ham will be ever lower than Shem; Shem will be ever lower than Japheth. All will rise in the Christian grandeur to be revealed. Ham will be lower than Shem, because he was sent to Central Africa. Man south of the Equator--in Asia, Australia, Oceanica, America, especially Africa--is inferior to his Northern brother. The blessing was upon Shem in his magnificent Asia. The greater blessing was upon Japheth in his man-developing Europe. Both blessings will be combined, in America, _north of the Zone_, in commingled light and life. I see it all in the first symbolical altar of Noah on that mound at the base of Ararat. The father of all living men bows before the incense of sacrifice, streaming up and mingling with the rays of the rising sun. His noble family, and all flesh saved, are grouped round about him. There is Ham, at the foot of the green hillock, standing, in his antediluvian, rakish recklessness, near the long-necked giraffe, type of his _Africa_,--his magnificent wife, seated on the grass, her little feet nestling in the tame lion's mane, her long black hair flowing over crimson drapery and covered with gems from mines before the flood. Higher up is Shem, leaning his arm over that mouse-colored horse,--his Arab steed. His wife, in pure white linen, feeds the elephant, and plays with his lithe proboscis,--the mother of Terah, Abraham, Isaac, Jacob, Joseph, David, and Christ. And yet she looks up, and bows in mild humility, to her of Japheth, seated amid plumed birds, in robes like the sky. Her noble lord, meanwhile, high above all, stands, with folded arms, following that eagle which wheels up towards Ararat, displaying his breast glittering with stars and stripes of scarlet and silver,--radiant heraldry, traced by the hand of God. Now he purifies his eye in the sun, and now he spreads his broad wings in symbolic flight to the _West_, until lost to the prophetic eye of Japheth, under the bow of splendors set that day in the cloud. God's covenant with man,--oh, may the bow of covenant between us be here to-day, that the waters of this flood shall never again threaten our beloved land!

Speech Delivered in the General Assembly New York, 1856.

The circumstances, under which this speech was delivered, are sufficiently shown in the statement below.

It was not a hasty production. After being spoken, it was prepared for the "Journal of Commerce," with the greatest care I could give to it: most of it was written again and again. Unlike Pascal, who said, as to his longest and inferior sixteenth letter, that he had not had time to make it shorter, I had time; and I did condense in that one speech the matured reflections of my whole life. I am calmly satisfied I am right. I am sure God has said, and does say, "Well done."

The speech brings to view a wide range of thought, all belonging to the subject of slavery, of immense importance. As introductory,--there is the question of the abolition agitation the last thirty years; then, what is right and wrong, and the foundation of moral obligation; then, the definition of sin; next, the origin of human government, and the relations, in which God has placed men under his rule of subjection; finally, the word of God is brought to sustain all the positions taken.

The challenge to argue the question of slavery from the Bible was thrown down on the floor of the Assembly, as stated. Presently I took up the gauntlet, and made this argument. The challenger never claimed his glove, then nor since; nor has anybody, so far as I know, attempted to refute this speech.

Nothing has come to my ears (save as to two points, to be noticed hereafter) but reckless, bold denial of God's truth, infidel affirmation without attempt at proof, and denunciations of myself.

Dr. Wisner having said that he would argue the question on the Bible at a following time, Dr. Ross rose, when he took his seat, and, taking his position on the platform near the Moderator's chair, said,--

"I accept the challenge given by Dr. Wisner, to argue the question of slavery from the Scriptures."

Dr. Wisner.--Does the brother propose to go into it here?

Dr. Ross.--Yes, sir.

Dr. Wisner.--Well, I did not propose to go into it here.

Dr. Ross.--You gave the challenge, and I accept it.

Dr. Wisner.--I said I would argue it at a proper time; but it is no matter. Go ahead.

Dr. Beman hoped the discussion would be ruled out. He did not think it a legitimate subject to go into,--Moses and the prophets, Christ and his apostles, and all intermediate authorities, on the subject of what the General Assembly of the Presbyterian Church in America had done.

Judge Jessup considered the question had been opened by this report of the majority: after which _Dr. Beman_ withdrew his objection, and _Dr. Ross_ proceeded.

I am not a slave-holder. Nay, I have shown some self-denial in that matter. I emancipated slaves whose money-value would now be $40,000. In the providence of God, my riches have entirely passed from me. I do not mean that, like the widow, I gave all the living I had. My estate was then greater than that slave-property. I merely wish to show I have no selfish motive in giving, as I shall, the true Southern defence of slavery. (Applause.) I speak from Huntsville, Alabama, my present home. That gem of the South, that beautiful city where the mountain softens into the vale,--where the water gushes, a great fountain, from the rock,--where around that living stream there are streets of roses, and houses of intelligence and gracefulness and gentlest hospitality,--and, withal, where so high honor is ever given to the ministers of God.

Speaking then from that region where "_Cotton is king_," I affirm, contrary as my opinion is to that most common in the South, that the slavery agitation has accomplished and will do great good. I said so, to ministerial and political friends, twenty-five years ago. I have always favored the agitation,--just as I have always countenanced discussion upon all subjects. I felt that the slavery question needed examination. I believed it was not understood in its relations to the Bible and human liberty. Sir, the light is spreading North and South. 'Tis said, I know, this agitation has increased the severity of slavery. True, but for a moment only, in the days of the years of the life of this noble problem. Farmers tell us that deep ploughing in poor ground will, for a year or two, give you a worse crop than before you went so deep; but that that deep ploughing will turn up the under-soil, and sun and air and rain will give you harvests increasingly rich. So, this moral soil, North and South, was unproductive. It needed deep ploughing. For a time the harvest was worse. Now it is becoming more and more abundant. The political controversy, however fierce and threatening, is only for power. But the moral agitation is for the harmony of the Northern and Southern mind, in the right interpretations of Scripture on this great subject, and, of course, for the ultimate union of the hearts of all sensible people, to fulfil God's intention,--to bless the white man and the black man in America. I am sure of this. I take a wide view of the progress of the destiny of this vast empire. I see God in America. I see him in the North and in the South. I see him more honored in the South to-day than he was twenty-five years ago; and that that higher regard is due, mainly, to the agitation of the slavery question. Do you ask how?

Why, sir, this is the how. Twenty-five years ago the religious mind of the South was leavened by wrong Northern training, on the great point of the right and wrong of slavery. Meanwhile, powerful intellects in the South, following the mere light of a healthy good sense, guided by the common grace of God, reached the very truth of this great matter,--namely, that the relation of the master and slave is not sin; and that, notwithstanding its admitted evils, it is a connection between the highest and the lowest races of man, revealing influences which may be, and will be, most benevolent for the ultimate good of the master and the slave,--conservative on the Union, by preserving the South from all forms of Northern fanaticism, and thereby being a great balance-wheel in the working of the tremendous machinery of our experiment of self-government. This seen result of slavery was found to be in absolute harmony with the word of God. These men, then, of highest grade of thought, who had turned in scorn from Northern notions, now see, in the Bible, that these notions are false and silly. They now read the Bible, never examined before, with growing respect. God is honored, and his glory will be more and more in their salvation. These are some of the moral consummations of this agitation in the South. The development has been twofold in the North. On the one hand, some anti-slavery men have left the light of the Bible, and wandered into the darkness until they have reached the blackness of the darkness of infidelity. Other some are following hard after, and are throwing the Bible into the furnace,--are melting it into iron, and forging it, and welding it, and twisting it, and grooving it into the shape and significance and goodness and gospel of Sharpe's rifles. Sir, are you not afraid that some of your once best men will soon have no better Bible than that?

But, on the other hand, many of your brightest minds are looking intensely at the subject, in the same light in which it is studied by the highest Southern reason. Ay, sir, mother-England, old fogy as she is, begins to open her eyes. What, then, is our gain? Sir, Uncle Tom's Cabin, in many of its conceptions, could not have been written twenty-five years ago. That book of genius,--over which I and hundreds in the world have freely wept,--true in all its facts, false in all its impressions,--yea, as false in the prejudice it creates to Southern social life as if Webster, the murderer of Parkman, may be believed to be a personification of the elite of honor in Cambridge, Boston, and New England. Nevertheless, Uncle Tom's Cabin could not have been written twenty-five years ago. Dr. Nehemiah Adams's "_South-Side View_" could not have been written twenty-five years ago. Nor Dr. Nathan Lord's "Letter of Inquiry." Nor Miss Murray's book. Nor "_Cotton is King_". Nor Bledsoe's "_Liberty and Slavery"_. These books, written in the midst of this agitation, are all of high, some the highest, reach of talent and noblest piety; all give, with increasing confidence, the present Southern Bible reading on Slavery. May the agitation, then, go on! I know the New School Presbyterian church has sustained some temporary injury. But God is honored in his word. The reaction, when the first abolition-movement commenced, has been succeeded by the sober second thought of the South. The sun, stayed, is again travelling in the greatness of his strength, and will shine brighter and brighter to the perfect day.

My only fear, Mr. Moderator, is that, as you Northern people are so prone to go to extremes in your zeal and run every thing into the ground, you may, perhaps, become _too pro-slavery;_ and that we may have to take measures against your coveting, over much, our daughters, if not our wives, our men-servants, our maid-servants, our houses, and our lands. (Laughter.)

Sir, I come now to the Bible argument. I begin at the beginning of eternity! (Laughter.) WHAT is RIGHT AND WRONG? _That's the question of questions_.

Two theories have obtained in the world. The one is, that right and wrong are eternal facts; that they exist per se in the nature of things; that they are ultimate truths above God; that he must study, and does study, to know them, as really as man. And that he comprehends them more clearly than man, only because he is a better student than man. Now, sir, this theory is atheism. For if right and wrong are like mathematical truths--fixed facts--then I may find them out, as I find out mathematical truths, without instruction from God. I do not ask God to tell me that one and one make two. I do not ask him to reveal to me the demonstrations of Euclid. I thank him for the mind to perceive. But I perceive mathematical relations without his telling me, because they exist independent of his will. If, then, moral truths, if right and wrong, if rectitude and sin, are, in like manner, fixed, eternal facts,--if they are out from and above God, like mathematical entities,--then I may find them for myself. I may condescend, perhaps, to regard the Bible as a hornbook, in which God, an older student than I, tells me how to begin to learn what he had to study; or I may decline to be taught, through the Bible, how to learn right and wrong. I may think the Bible was good enough, may be, for the Israelite in Egypt and in Canaan; good enough for the Christian in Jerusalem and Antioch and Rome, but not good enough, even as a hornbook, for me,--the man of the nineteenth century,--the man of Boston, New York, and Brooklyn! Oh, no. I may think I need it not at all. What next? Why, sir, if I may think I need not God to teach me moral truth, I may think I need him not to teach me any thing. What next? The irresistible conclusion is, I may think I can live without God; that Jehovah is a myth,--a name; I may bid him stand aside, or die. Oh, sir, I will be the fool to say there is no God. This is the result of the notion that right and wrong exist in the nature of things.

The other theory is, that right and wrong are results brought into being, mere contingencies, means to good, made to exist solely by the will of God, expressed through his word; or, when his will is not thus known, he shows it in the human reason by which he rules the natural heart. This is so; because God, in making all things, saw that in the relations he would constitute between himself and intelligent creatures, and among themselves, NATURAL GOOD AND EVIL would come to pass. In his benevolent wisdom, he then willed LAW, to control this natural good and evil. And he thereby made conformity to that law to be _right_, and _non-conformity_ to be wrong. Why? Simply because he saw it to be good, and made it to be right; not because _he saw it to be right_, but because he made it to be right.

Hence, the ten specific commandments of the one moral law of love are just ten rules which God made to regulate the natural good and evil which he knew would be in the ten relations, which he himself constituted between himself and man, and between man and his neighbor. The Bible settles the question:--_sin is the transgression of the law, and where there is no law there is no sin_.

I must-advance one step further. _What is sin_, as a mental state? Is it some quality--some concentrated essence--some elementary moral particle in the nature of things--something black, or red, like crimson, in the constitution of the soul, or the soul and body as amalgamated? No. Is it self-love? No. Is it selfishness? No. What is it? Just exactly, _self-will._ Just that. I, the creature, WILL not submit to thy WILL, God, the Creator. It is the I AM, _created_, who dares to defy and dishonor the I AM, not created,--the Lord God, the Almighty, Holy, Eternal.

That IS SIN, per se. And that is all of it,--so help me God! Your child there--John--says to his father, "I WILL not to submit to your will." "Why not, John?" And he answers and says, "Because I WILL not." There, sir, John has revealed _all of sin_, on earth or in hell. Satan has never said--can never say--more. "I, Satan, WILL NOT, because I WILL not to submit to thee, God; MY WILL, not thine, shall be."

This beautiful theory is the ray of light which leads us from night, and twilight, and fog, and mist, and mystification, on this subject, to clear day. I will illustrate it by the law which has controlled and now regulates the most delicate of all the relations of life,--viz.: that of the intercourse between the sexes. I take this, because it presents the strongest apparent objections to my argument.

Cain and Abel married their sisters. Was it wrong in the nature of things? [Here Dr. Wisner spoke out, and said, "Certainly."] I deny it. What an absurdity, to suppose that God could not provide for the propagation of the human race from one pair, without _requiring them to sin!_ Adam's sons and daughters must have married, had they remained in innocence. They must then have sinned in Eden, from the very necessity of the command upon the race:--"Be fruitful, and multiply, and replenish the earth." (Gen. i. 28). What pure nonsense! There, sir!--_that_, my one question, Dr. Wisner's reply, and my rejoinder, bring out, perfectly, the two theories of right and wrong. Sir,

Abraham married his half-sister. And there is not a word forbidding such marriage, until God gave the law (Lev. xviii.) prohibiting marriage in certain degrees of consanguinity. That law made, then, such marriage sin. But God gave no such law in the family of Adam; because he made, himself, the marriage of brother and sister the way, and the only way, for the increase of the human race. _He commanded them thus to marry. They would have sinned had they not thus married_; for they would have transgressed his law. Such marriage was not even a natural evil, in the then family of man. But when, in the increase of numbers, it became a natural evil, physical and social, God placed man on a higher platform for the development of civilization, morals, and religion, and then made the law regulating marriages in the particulars of blood. But he still left polygamy untouched. [Here Dr. Wisner again asked if Dr. R. regarded the Bible as sustaining the polygamy of the Old Testament.] Dr. R.--Yes, sir; yes, sir; yes, sir. Let the reporters mark that question, and my answer. (Laughter.) My principle vindicates God from unintelligible abstractions. I fearlessly tell what the Bible says. In its strength, I am not afraid of earth or hell. I fear only God. God made no law against polygamy, in the beginning. Therefore it was no sin for a man to have more wives than one. God sanctioned it, and made laws in regard to it. Abraham had more wives than one; Jacob had, David had, Solomon had. God told David, by the mouth of Nathan, when he upbraided him with his ingratitude for the blessings he had given him, and said, "And I gave thee thy master's house, and _thy master's wives_ into thy bosom." (2 Sam. xvii. 8.)

God, in the gospel, places man on another platform, for the revelation of a nobler social and spiritual life. He now forbids polygamy. _Polygamy now is sin_--not because it is in itself sin. No; but because God forbids it,--to restrain the natural and social evil, and to bring out a higher humanity. And see, sir, how gently in the gospel the transition from the lower to the higher table-land of our progress upward is made. Christ and his apostles do not declare polygamy to be sin. The new law is so wisely given that nothing existing is rudely disturbed. The minister of God, unmarried, must have only one wife at the same time. This law, silently and gradually, by inevitable and fair inference of its meaning, and from the example of the apostles, passed over the Christian world. God, in the gospel, places us in this higher and holier ground and air of love. We sin, then, if we marry the sister, and other near of kin; and we sin if we marry, at the same time, more wives than one, not because there is sin in the thing itself, whatever of natural evil there might be, but because in so doing we transgress God's law, given to secure and advance the good of man. I might comment in the same way on every one of the ten commandments, but I pass on.

The subject of slavery, in this view of _right and wrong_, is seen in the very light of heaven. And you, Mr. Moderator, know that, if the view I have presented be true, I have got you. (Great laughter.)

[The Moderator said, very pleasantly--Yes--_if_--but it is a long if.] (Continued laughter.)

Dr. R. touched the Moderator on the shoulder, and said, Yes, _if_--it is a _long if_; for it is this:--if there is a God, he is not Jupiter, bowing to the Fates, but God, the sovereign over the universe he has created, in which he makes right, by making law to be known and obeyed by angels and men, in their varied conditions.

He gave Adam that command,--sublime in its simplicity, and intended to vindicate the principle I am affirming,--that there is no right and wrong in the nature of things. There was no right or wrong, _per se_, in eating or willing to eat of that tree of the knowledge of good and evil.

But God made the law,--Thou shall not eat of that tree. As if he had said,--I seek to test the submission of your will, freely, to my will. And, that your test may be perfect, I will let your temptation be nothing more than your natural desire for that fruit. Adam sinned. What was the sin?

Adam said, in heart, MY WILL, _not thine_, SHALL BE. That was the sin,--_the simple transgression of God's law_, when there was neither sin nor evil in the thing which God forbade to be done.

Man fell and was cursed. The law of the control of the superior over the inferior is now to begin, and is to go on in the depraved conditions of the fallen and cursed race. And, FIRST, God said to the woman, "_Thy desire shall be to thy husband, and he shall rule over thee." There,_ in that law, is _the beginning of government ordained of God. There_ is the beginning of the rule of the superior over the inferior, bound to obey. _There_, in the family of Adam, is the germ of the rule in the tribe,--the state. Adam, in his right, from God, to rule over his wife and his children, had all the authority afterwards expanded in the patriarch and the king. This simple, beautiful fact, there, on the first leaf of the Bible, solves the problem, whence and how has man right to rule over man. In that great fact God gives his denial to the idea that government over man is the result of a social compact, in which each individual man living in a state of natural liberty, yielded some of that liberty to secure the greater good of government. Such a thing never was; such a thing never could have been. _Government was ordained and established before the first child was born:_--"HE SHALL RULE OVER THEE." Cain and Abel were born in a state as perfect as the empire of Britain or the rule of these United States. All that Blackstone, and Paley, and Hobbs, or anybody else, says about the social compact, is flatly and fully denied and upset by the Bible, history, and common sense. Let any New York lawyer--or even a Philadelphia lawyer--deny this if he dares. _Life, liberty, and the pursuit of happiness_ never were the inalienable right of the individual man.

His self-control, in all these particulars, _from the beginning_, was subordinate to the good of the family,--the empire. The command to Noah was,--"Whoso sheddeth man's blood, by man shall his blood be shed." (Gen. ix. 6.)

This command to shed blood was, and is, in perfect harmony with the law,--"Thou shalt not kill." There is nothing right or wrong in _the taking of life_, per se, or in itself considered. It may or it may not be a natural good or evil. As a _general fact_, the taking of life is a natural evil. Hence, "Thou shalt not kill" is the general rule, to preserve the good there is in life. To take life under the forbidden conditions is sin, simply because God forbids it under those conditions. The sin is not in taking life, but in transgressing God's law.

But sometimes the taking of life will secure a greater good. God, then, commands that life be taken. Not to take life, under the commanded conditions, is sin,--solely because God then commands it.

This power over life, for the good of the one great family of man, God delegated to Noah, and through him to the tribe, the clan, the kingdom, the empire, the democracy, the republic, as they may be governed by chief, king, emperor, parliament, or congress. Had Ham killed Shem, Noah would have commanded Japheth to slay him. So much for the origin of the power over life: now for the power over liberty.

The right to take life included the right over liberty. But God intended the rule of the superior over the inferior, in relations of service, should _exemplify human depravity, his curse and his overruling blessing_.

The rule and the subordination which is essential to the existence of the family, God made commensurate with mankind; for mankind is only the congeries of families. When Ham, in his antediluvian recklessness, laughed at his father, God took occasion to give to the world the rule of the superior over the inferior. _He cursed him. He cursed him because he left him unblessed_. The withholding of the father's blessing, in the Bible, was curse. Hence Abraham prayed God, when Isaac was blessed, that Ishmael might not be passed by. Hence Esau prayed his father, when Jacob was blessed, that he might not be left untouched by his holy hands. Ham was cursed to render service, forever, to Shem and Japheth. The special curse on Canaan made the general curse on Ham conspicuous, historic, and explanatory, simply because his descendants were to be brought under the control of God's peculiar people. Shem was blessed to rule over Ham. Japheth was blessed to rule over both. God sent Ham to Africa, Shem to Asia, Japheth to Europe. Mr. Moderator, you have read Guyot's "Earth and Man." That admirable book is a commentary upon this part of Genesis. It is the philosophy of geography. And it is the philosophy of the rule of the higher races over the inferior, written on the very face of the earth. He tells you why the continents are shaped as they are shaped; why the mountains stand where they stand; why the rivers run where they run; why the currents of the sea and the air flow as they flow. And he tells you that the earth south of the Equator makes the inferior man. That the oceanic climate makes the inferior man in the Pacific Islands. That South America makes the inferior man. That the solid, unindented Southern Africa makes the inferior man. That the huge, heavy, massive, magnificent Asia makes the huge, heavy, massive, magnificent man. That Europe, indented by the sea on every side, with its varied scenery, and climate, and Northern influences, makes the varied intellect, the versatile power and life and action, of the master-man of the world. And it is so. Africa, with here and there an exception, has never produced men to compare with the men of Asia. For six thousand years, save the unintelligible stones of Egypt, she has had no history. Asia has had her great men and her name. But Europe has ever shown, and now, her nobler men and higher destiny. Japheth has now come to North America, to give us his past greatness and his transcendent glory. (Applause.) And, sir, I thank God our mountains stand where they stand; and that our rivers run where they run. Thank God they run not across longitudes, but across latitudes, from north to south. If they crossed longitudes, we might fear for the Union. But I hail the Union,--made by God, strong as the strength of our hills, and ever to live and expand,--like the flow and swell of the current of our streams. (Applause.)

These two theories of Right and Wrong,--these two ideas of human liberty,--the right, in the nature of things, or the right as made by God,--the liberty of the individual man, of Atheism, of Red Republicanism, of the devil,--or the liberty of man, in the family, in the State, the liberty from God,--these two theories now make the conflict of the world. This anti-slavery battle is only part of the great struggle: God will be victorious,--and we, in his might.

I now come to particular illustrations of the world-wide law that service shall be rendered by the inferior to the superior. The relations in which such service obtains are very many. Some of them are these:--husband and wife;

parent and child; teacher and scholar; commander and soldier,--sailor; master and apprentice; master and hireling; master and slave. Now, sir, all these relations are ordained of God. They are all directly commanded, or they are the irresistible law of his providence, in conditions which must come up in the progress of depraved nature. The relations themselves are all good in certain conditions. And there may be no more of evil in the lowest than in the highest. And there may be in the lowest, as really as in the highest, the fulfilment of the commandment to love thy neighbor as thyself, and of doing unto him whatsoever thou wouldst have him to do unto thee.

Why, sir, the wife everywhere, except where Christianity has given her elevation, is the slave. And, sir, I say, without fear of saying too strongly, that for every sigh, every groan, every tear, every agony of stripe or death, which has gone up to God from the relation of master and slave, there have been more sighs, more groans, more tears, and more agony in the rule of the husband over the wife. Sir, I have admitted, and do again admit, without qualification, that every fact in Uncle Tom's Cabin has occurred in the South. But, in reply, I say deliberately, what one of your first men told me, that he who will make the horrid examination will discover in New York City, in any number of years past, more cruelty from husband to wife, parent to child, than in all the South from master to slave in the same time. I dare the investigation. And you may extend it further, if you choose,--to all the results of honor and purity. I fear nothing on this subject. I stand on rock,--the Bible,--and therefore, just before I bring the Bible, to which all I have said is introductory, I will run a parallel between the relation of master and slave and that of husband and wife. I will say nothing of the grinding oppression of capital upon labor, in the power of the master over the hireling--the crushed peasant--the chain-harnessed coal-pit woman, a thousand feet under ground, working in darkness, her child toiling by her side, and another child not born; I will say nothing of the press-gang which fills the navy of Britain--the conscription which makes the army of France--the terrible floggings--the awful court-martial--the quick sentence--the lightning-shot--the chain, and ball, and every-day lash--the punishment of the soldier, sailor, slave, who had run away. I pass all this by: I will run the parallel between the slave and wife.

Do you say, The slave is held to _involuntary service?_ So is the wife. Her relation to her husband, in the immense majority of cases, is made for her, and not by her. And when she makes it for herself, how often, and how soon, does it become involuntary! How often, and how soon, would she throw off the yoke if she could! O ye wives, I know how superior you are to your husbands in many respects,--not only in personal attraction, (although in that particular, comparison is out of place,) in grace, in refined thought, in passive fortitude, in enduring love, and in a heart to be filled with the spirit of heaven. Oh, I know all this. Nay, I know you may surpass him in his own sphere of boasted prudence and worldly wisdom about dollars and cents. Nevertheless, he has authority, from God, to rule over you. You are under service to him. You are bound to obey him in all things. Your service is very, very, very often involuntary from the first, and, if voluntary at first, becomes hopeless necessity afterwards. I know God has laid upon the husband to love you as Christ loved the church, and in that sublime obligation has placed you in the light and under the shadow of a love infinitely higher, and purer, and holier than all talked about in the romances of chivalry. But the husband may not so love you. He may rule you with the rod of iron. What can you do? Be divorced? God forbids it, save for crime. Will you say that you are free,--that you will go where you please, do as you please? Why, ye dear wives, your husbands may forbid. And listen, you cannot leave New York, nor your palaces, any more than your shanties. No; you cannot leave your parlor, nor your bedchamber, nor your couch, if your husband commands you to stay there! What can you do? Will you run away, with your stick and your bundle? He can advertise you!! What can you do? You can, and I fear some of you do, wish him, from the bottom of your hearts, at the bottom of the Hudson. Or, in your self-will, you will do just as you please. (Great laughter.)

[A word on the subject of divorce. One of your standing denunciations on the South is the terrible laxity of the marriage vow among the slaves. Well, sir, what does your Boston Dr. Nehemiah Adams say? He says, after giving eighty, sixty, and the like number of applications for divorce, and nearly all granted at individual quarterly courts in New England,--he says he is not sure but that the marriage relation is as enduring among the slaves in the South as it is among white people in New England. I only give what Dr. Adams says. I would fain vindicate the marriage relation from this rebuke. But one thing I will say: you seldom hear of a divorce in Virginia or South Carolina.]

But to proceed:--

Do you say the slave is _sold and bought?_ So is the wife the world over. Everywhere, always, and now as the general fact, however done away or modified by Christianity. The savage buys her. The barbarian buys her. The Turk buys her. The Jew buys her. The Christian buys her,--Greek, Armenian, Nestorian, Roman Catholic, Protestant. The Portuguese, the Spaniard, the Italian, the German, the Russian, the Frenchman, the Englishman, the New England man, the New Yorker,--especially the upper ten,--_buy the wife_--in many, very many cases. She is seldom bought in the South, and never among the slaves themselves; for they always marry for love. (Continued laughter.) Sir, I say the wife is bought in the highest circles, too often, as really as the slave is bought. Oh, she is not sold and purchased in the public market. But come, sir, with me, and let us take the privilege of spirits out of the body to glide into that gilded saloon, or into that richly comfortable family room, of cabinets, and pictures, and statuary: see the parties, there, to sell and buy that human body and soul, and make her a chattel! See how they sit, and bend towards each other, in earnest colloquy, on sofa of rosewood and satin,--Turkey carpet (how befitting!) under feet, sunlight over head, softened through stained windows: or it is night, and the gas is turned nearly off, and the burners gleam like stars through the shadow from which the whisper is heard, in which that old ugly brute, with gray goatee--how fragrant!--bids one, two, five, ten hundred thousand dollars, and she is knocked off to him,--that beautiful young girl asleep up there, amid flowers, and innocent that she is sold and bought. Sir, that young girl would as soon permit a baboon to embrace her, as that old, ignorant, gross, disgusting wretch to approach her. Ah, has she not been sold and bought for money? But--But what? But, you say, she freely, and without parental authority, accepted him. Then she sold herself for money, and was guilty of that which is nothing better than legal prostitution. I know what I say; you know what I say. Up there in the gallery you know: you nod to one another. Ah! you know the parties. Yes, you say: All true, true, true. (Laughter.)

Now, Mr. Moderator, I will clinch all I have said by nails sure, and fastened from the word of God.

There is King James's English Bible, with its magnificent dedication. I bring the English acknowledged translation. And just one word more to push gently aside--for I am a kind man to those poor, deluded anti-slavery people--their last argument. It is that this English Bible, in those parts which treat of slavery, don't give the ideas which are found in the original Hebrew and Greek. Alas for the common people!--alas for this good old translation! Are its days numbered? No, sir; no, sir. The Unitarian, the Universalist, the Arminian, the Baptist, when pressed by this translation, have tried to find shelter for their false isms by making or asking for a new rendering. And now the anti-slavery men are driving hard at the same thing. (Laughter.) Sir, shall we permit our people everywhere to have their confidence in this noble translation undermined and destroyed by the isms and whims of every or any man in our pulpits? I affirm, whatever be our perfect liberty of examination into God's meaning in all the light of the original languages, that there is a respect due to this received version, and that great caution should be used, lest we teach the people to doubt its true rendering from the original word of God. I protest, sir, against having a Doctor-of-Divinity _priest_, Hebrew or Greek, to tell the people what God has spoken on the subject of slavery or any other subject. (Laughter.) I would as soon have a Latin priest,--I would as soon have Archbishop Hughes,--I would as soon go to Rome as to Jerusalem or Athens,--I would as soon have the Pope at once in his fallible infallibility,--as ten or twenty, little or big, anti-slavery Doctor-of-Divinity priests, each claiming to give his infallible rendering, however differing from his peer. (Laughter.) I never yet produced this Bible, in its plain unanswerable authority, for the relation of master and slave, but the anti-slavery man ran away into the fog of his Hebrew or Greek, (laughter,) or he jabbered the nonsense that God permitted the sin of slaveholding among the Jews, but that he don't do it now!

Sir, God sanctioned slavery then, and sanctions it now. He made it right, they know, then and now. Having thus taken the last puff of wind out of the sails of the anti-slavery phantom ship, turn to the twenty-first chapter of Exodus, vs. 2-5. God, in these verses, gave the Israelites his command how they should buy and hold the Hebrew servant,--how, under certain conditions, he went free,--how, under other circumstances, he might be held to service forever, with his wife and her children. There it is. Don't run into the Hebrew. (Laughter.)

But what have we here?--vs. 7-11:--"And if a man sell his daughter to be a maid-servant, she shall not go out as the men-servants do. If she please not her master, who hath betrothed her to himself, then shall he let her be redeemed: to sell her unto a strange nation he shall have no power, seeing he hath dealt deceitfully with her. And if he hath betrothed her unto his son, he shall deal with her after the manner of daughters. If he take him another wife, her food, her raiment, and her duty of marriage shall he not diminish. And if he do not these three unto her, then shall she go out free without money." Now, sir, the wit of man can't dodge that passage, unless he runs away into the Hebrew. (Great laughter.) For what does God say? Why, this:--that an Israelite might sell his own daughter, not only into servitude, but into polygamy,--that the buyer might, if he pleased, give her to his son for a wife, or take her to himself. If he took her to himself, and she did not please him, he should not sell her unto a strange nation, but should allow her to be redeemed by her family. But, if he took him another wife before he allowed the first one to be redeemed, he should continue to give the first one _food_, her _raiment_, and her _duty of marriage_; that is to say, her right to his bed. If he did not do _these three things_, she should go out free; _i.e._ cease to be his slave, without his receiving any money for her. There, sir, God sanctioned the Israelite father in selling his daughter, and the Israelite man to buy her, into slavery and into polygamy. And it was then right, because God made it right. In verses 20 and 21, you have these words:--"And if a man smite his servant or his maid with a rod, and he die under his hand, he shall be surely punished; notwithstanding, if he continue a day or two, he shall not be punished: for he is his money." What does this passage mean? Surely this:-

-if the master gave his slave a hasty blow with a rod, and he died under his hand, he should be punished. But, if the slave lived a day or two, it would so extenuate the act of the master he should not be punished, inasmuch as he would be in that case sufficiently punished in losing his money in his slave. Now, sir, I affirm that God was more lenient to the degraded Hebrew master than Southern laws are to the higher Southern master in like cases. But there you have what was the divine will. Find fault with God, ye anti-slavery men, if you dare. In Leviticus, xxv. 44-46, "Both thy bondmen and thy bondmaids, which thou shalt have, shall be of the heathen that are round about you; of them shall ye buy bondmen and bondmaids. Moreover, of the children of the strangers that do sojourn among you, of them shall ye buy, and of their families that are with you, which they beget in your land: and they shall be your possession. And ye shall take them as an inheritance for your children after you, to inherit them for a possession; they shall be your bondmen forever."

Sir, I do not see how God could tell us more plainly that he did command his people to buy slaves from the heathen round about them, and from the stranger, and of their families sojourning among them. The passage has no other meaning. Did God merely permit sin?--did he merely tolerate a dreadful evil? God does not say so anywhere. He gives his people law to buy and hold slaves of the heathen forever, on certain conditions, and to buy and hold Hebrew slaves in variously-modified particulars. Well, how did the heathen, then, get slaves to sell? Did they capture them in war?--did they sell their own children? Wherever they got them, they sold them; and God's law gave his people the right to buy them.

God in the New Testament made no law prohibiting the relation of master and slave. But he made law regulating the relation under Greek and Roman slavery, which was the most oppressive in the world.

God saw that these regulations would ultimately remove the evils in the Greek and Roman systems, and do it away entirely from the fitness of things, as there existing; for Greek and Roman slaves, for the most part, were the equals in all respects of their masters. Aesop was a slave; Terence was a slave. The precepts in Colossians iv. 18, 23, 1 Tim. vi. 1-6, and other places, show, unanswerably, that God as really sanctioned the relation of master and slave as those of husband and wife, and parent and child; and that all the obligations of the moral law, and Christ's law of love, might and must be as truly fulfilled in the one relation as in the other. The fact that he has made the one set of relations permanent, and the other more or less dependent on conditions of mankind, or to pass away in the advancement of human progress, does not touch the question. He sanctioned it under the Old Testament and the New, and ordains it now while he sees it best to continue it, and he now, as heretofore, proclaims the duty of the master and the slave. Dr. Parker's admirable explanation of Colossians, and other New Testament passages, saves me the necessity of saying any thing more on the Scripture argument.

One word on the Detroit resolutions, and I conclude. Those resolutions of the Assembly of 1850 decide that slavery is sin, unless the master holds his slave as a guardian, or under the claims of humanity.

Mr. Moderator, I think we had on this floor, yesterday, proof conclusive that those resolutions mean any thing or nothing; that they are a fine specimen of Northern skill in platform-making; that it put in a plank here, to please this man,--a plank there, to please that man,--a plank for the North, a broad board for the South. It is Jackson's judicious tariff. It is a gum-elastic conscience, stretched now to a charity covering all the multitude of our Southern sins, contracted now, giving us hardly a fig-leaf of righteousness. It is a bowl of punch,--

A little sugar to make it sweet, A little lemon to make it sour, A little water to make it weak, A little brandy to give it power. (Laughter.)

As a Northern argument against us, it is a mass of lead so heavy that it weighed down even the strong shoulders of Judge Jessup. For, sir, when he closed his speech, I asked him a single question I had made ready for him. It was this:--"Do you allow that Mr. Aiken, of South Carolina, may, under the claims of humanity, hold three thousand slaves, or must he emancipate them?" The Judge staggered, and stammered, and said, "No man could rightly hold so many." I then asked, "How many may he hold, in humanity?" The Judge saw his fatal dilemma. He recovered himself handsomely, and fairly said, "Mr. Aiken might hold three thousand slaves, in harmony with the Detroit action." I replied, "Then, sir, you have surrendered the whole question of Southern slavery." And, sir, the Judge looked as if he felt he had surrendered it. And every man in this house, capable of understanding the force of that question, felt it had shivered the whole anti-slavery argument, on those resolutions, to atoms. Why, sir, if a man can hold three slaves, with a right heart and the approbation of God, he may hold thirty, three hundred, three thousand, or thirty thousand. It is a mere question of heart, and capacity to govern. The Emperor of Russia holds sixty millions of slaves: and is there a man in this house so much of a fool as to say that God regards the Emperor of Russia a sinner because he is the master of sixty millions of slaves? Sir, that Emperor has certainly a high and awful responsibility upon him. But, if he is good as he is great, he is a god of benevolence on earth. And so is every Southern master. His obligation is high, and great, and glorious. It is the same obligation, in kind, he is under to his wife and children, and in some respects immensely higher, by reason of the number and the tremendous interests involved for time and eternity in connection with this great country, Africa, and the world. Yes, sir, _I know_, whether Southern masters fully know it or not, that _they hold from God_, individually and collectively, _the highest and the noblest responsibility ever given by Him to individual private men on all the face of the earth._ For God has intrusted to them to train millions of the most degraded in form and intellect, but, at the same time, the most gentle, the most amiable, the most affectionate, the most imitative, the most susceptible of social and religious love, of all the races of mankind,-- to train them, and to give them civilization, and the light and the life of the gospel of Jesus Christ. And I thank God he has given this great work to that type of the noble family of Japheth best qualified to do it,--to the Cavalier stock,--the gentleman and the lady of England and France, born to command, and softened and refined under our Southern sky. May they know and feel and fulfil their destiny! Oh, may they "know that they also have a Master in heaven."

Letter from Dr. Ross.

I need only say, in reference to this letter, that my friends having questioned my position as to the good of the agitation, I wrote the following letter to vindicate that point, as given, in the New York speech:--

HUNTSVILLE, ALA., July 14, 1856.

Brother Blackburn:--I affirmed, in my New York speech, that the Slavery agitation has done, and will accomplish, good.

Your very kind and courteous disagreement on that point I will make the occasion to say something more thereon, without wishing you, my dear friend, to regard what I write as inviting any discussion.

I said that agitation has brought out, and would reveal still more fully, the Bible, in its relation to slavery and liberty,--also the infidelity which long has been, and is now, leavening with death the whole Northern mind. And that it would result in the triumph of the true Southern interpretation of the Bible; to the honor of God, and to the good of the master, the slave, the stability of the Union, and be a blessing to the world. To accomplish this, the sin per se doctrine will be utterly demolished. That doctrine is the difficulty in every _Northern mind,_ (where there is any difficulty about slavery,) whether they confess it or not. Yes, the difficulty with every Northern man is, that the relation of master and slave is felt to be sin. I know that to be the fact. I have talked with all grades of Northern men, and come in contact with all varieties of Northern mind on this subject. And I know that the man who says and tries to believe, and does, partially in sober judgment, believe, that slavery is not sin, yet, _in his feelings, in his educated prejudices_, he feels that slavery is sin.

Yes, that is the difficulty, and that is the whole of the difficulty, _between the North and the South_, so far as the question is one of the Bible and morals. Now, I again say, that that sin per se doctrine will, in this agitation, be utterly demolished. And when that is done,--when the North will know and feel fully, perfectly, that the relation of master and slave is not sin, but sanctioned of God,--then, and not till then, the North and South can and will, without anger, consider the following questions:--Whether slavery, as it exists in the United States, all things considered, be or be not a great good, and the greatest good for a time, notwithstanding its admitted evils? Again, whether these evils can or cannot be modified and removed? Lastly, whether slavery itself can or cannot pass away from this land and the world? Now, sir, the moment the sin question is settled, then all is peace. For these other questions belong entirely to another category of morals. They belong entirely to the category of what is wise to realize good. This agitation will bring this great result. And therefore I affirm the agitation to be good.

  There is another fact also, the result, in great measure, of this agitation, which in my view proves it to have been and to be of great good. I mean the astonishing rise and present stability of the slave-power of the United States. This fact, when examined, is undeniable. And it is equally undeniable that it has been caused, in great part, by the slavery question in all its bearings. It is a wonderful development made by God. And I must believe he intends thereby either to destroy or bless this great Union. But, as I believe he intends to bless, therefore I am fortified in affirming the good there has been and is in this agitation. Let me bring out to view this astonishing fact.

  1. Twenty-five years ago, and previously, the whole slave-holding South and West had a strong tendency to emancipation, in some form. But the abolition movement then began, and arrested that Southern and Western leaning to emancipation. Many people have said, and do say, that that arrest was and is a great evil. I say it was and is a great good. Why? Answer: It was and would now be premature. Had it been carried out, it would have been and would now be evil, immense, inconceivable,--to master, slave, America, Africa, and the world; because neither master, slave, America, Africa, the world, were, or

are, ready for emancipation. God has a great deal to do before he is ready for emancipation. He tells us so by this arrest put upon that tendency to emancipation years ago. For He put it into the hearts of abolitionists to make the arrest. And He stopped the Southern movement all the more perfectly by permitting Great Britain to emancipate Jamaica, and letting that experiment prove, as it has, a perfect failure and a terrible warning. JAMAICA IS DESTROYED. And now, whatever be done for its negroes must be done with the full admission that what has been attempted was in violation of the duty Britain owed to those negroes. But her failure in seeing and doing her duty, God has given to us to teach us knowledge; and, through us, to instruct the world in the demonstration of the problem of slavery.

2. God put it into the hearts of Northern men--especially abolitionists--to give Texas to the South. Texas, a territory so vast that a bird, as Webster said, can't fly over it in a week. Many in the South did not want Texas. But many longer-headed ones did want it. And Northern men voted and gave to the South exactly what these longer-headed Southern statesmen wanted. This, I grant, was Northern anti-slavery fatuity, utterly unaccountable but that God made them do it.

3. God put it into the hearts of Northern men--especially abolitionists--to vote for Polk, Dallas, and Texas. This gave us the Mexican War; and that immense territory, its spoil,--a territory which, although it may not be favorable for slave-labor, has increased, and will, in many ways, extend the slave-power.

4. This leads me to say that God put it into the hearts of many Northern men--especially abolitionists--to believe what Great Britain said,--namely, that free trade would result in slave-emancipation. _But lo! the slave-holder wanted free trade_. So Northern abolitionists helped to destroy the _tariff policy_, and thus to expand the demand for, and the culture of, cotton. Now, see, the gold of California has perpetuated free trade by enabling our merchants to meet the enormous demand for specie created by free trade. So California helps the slave-power. But the abolitionists gave us Polk, the

Mexican War, and California.

5. God put it into the hearts of the North, and especially abolitionists, to stimulate the settlement of new free States, and to be the ardent friends of an immense foreign emigration. The result has been to send down to the South, with railroad speed and certainty, corn, wheat, flour, meal, bacon, pork, beef, and every other imaginable form of food, in quantity amazing, and so cheap that the planter can spread wider and wider the culture of cotton.

6. God has, by this growth of the Northwest, made the demand for cotton enormous in the North and Northwest. Again, he has made English and French experiments to procure cotton somewhere else than from the United States _dead failures_,--in the East Indies, Egypt, Algeria, Brazil. God has thus given to the Southern planter an absolute monopoly. A monopoly so great that he, the Southern planter, sits now upon his throne of cotton and wields the commercial sceptre of the world. Yes, it is the Southern planter who says to-day to haughty England, Go to war, if you dare; dismiss Dallas, if you dare. Yes, he who sits on the throne of the cotton-bag has triumphed at last over him who sits on the throne of the wool-sack. England is prostrate at his feet, as well as the abolitionists.

7. God has put it into the hearts of abolitionists to prevent half a million of free negroes from going to Liberia; and thereby the abolitionists have made them consumers of slave-products to the extension of the slave-power. And, by thus keeping them in America, the abolitionists have so increased their degradation as to prove all the more the utter folly of emancipation in the United States.

8. God has permitted the anti-slavery men in the North, in England, in France, and everywhere, so to blind themselves in hypocrisy as to give the Southern slave-holder his last perfect triumph over them; for God tells the planter to say to the North, to England, to France, to all who buy cotton, "Ye men of Boston, New York, London, Paris,--ye hypocrites,--ye brand me as a pirate, a kidnapper, a murderer, a demon, fit only for hell, and yet ye buy my

blood-stained cotton. O ye hypocrites!--ye Boston hypocrites! why don't ye throw the cotton in the sea, as your fathers did the tea? Ye Boston hypocrites! ye say, _if we had been in the days of our fathers, we would not have been partakers with them in the blood of the slave-trade!_ Wherefore ye be witnesses unto yourselves that ye are the children of them who, in fact, kidnapped and bought in blood, and sold the slave in America! for now, ye hypocrites, ye buy the blood-stained cotton in quantity so immense, that ye have run up the price of slaves to be more than a thousand dollars,--the average of old and young! O ye hypocrites! ye denounce slavery; then ye bid it live, and not die,--in that ye buy sugar, rice, tobacco, and, above all, cotton! Ye hypocrites! ye abuse the devil, and then fall down and worship him!--ye hypocrites,--ye New England hypocrites,--ye Old England hypocrites,--ye French hypocrites,--ye Uncle Tom's Cabin hypocrites,--ye Beecher hypocrites,--ye Rhode Island Consociation hypocrites! Oh, your holy twaddle stinks in the nostrils of God, and he commands me to lash you with my scorn, and his scorn, so long as ye gabble about the sin of slavery, and then bow down to me, and buy and spin cotton, and thus work for me as truly as my slaves! O ye fools and blind, fill ye up the measure of your folly, and blindness, and shame! And this ye are doing. Ye have, like the French infidels, made reason your goddess, and are exalting her above the Bible; and, in your unitarianism and neology and all modes of infidelity, ye are rejecting and crucifying the Son of God."

Now, my brother, this controlling slave-power is a world-wide fact. Its statistics of bales count by millions; its tonnage counts by hundreds of thousands; its manufacture is reckoned by the workshops of America and Europe; its supporters are numbered by all who must thus be clothed in the world. This tremendous power has been developed in great measure by the abolition agitation, controlled by God. I believe, then, as I have already said, that God intends one of two things. He either intends to destroy the United States by this slave-power, or he intends to bless my country and the world by the unfoldings of his wisdom in this matter. I believe he will bless the world in the working out of this slavery. I rejoice, then, in the agitation which has so resulted, and will so terminate, to reveal the Bible, and bless mankind.

Your affectionate friend,

F.A. Ross.

REV. A. BLACKBURN.

What Is the Foundation of Moral Obligation?

My position as to this all-important question, in my New York speech, was made subject of remark in the "Presbyterian Herald," Louisville, Kentucky, to which I replied at length in the "Presbyterian Witness," Knoxville, Tennessee. No rejoinder was ever made to that reply. But, recently, an extract from the younger Edwards was submitted to me. To that I gave the following letter. The subject is of the first and the last importance, and bears directly, as set forth in my New York speech, on infidelity, and, of course, the slavery question:--

Mr. Editor:--In your paper of Tuesday, 24th ult., there is an article, under this head, giving the argument of Edwards (the son) against my views as to the foundation of moral obligation.

I thank the writer for his argument, and his courteous manner of presenting it. In my third letter to Mr. Barnes, I express my preparation to meet "_all comers_" on this question; and I am pleased to see this "_comer_". If my views cannot be refuted by Edwards, I may wait long for an "uglier customer."

A word, introductory, to your correspondent. He says, "His [Dr. Ross's] theory was advanced and argued against in a former age." By this, I understand him to express his belief that my theory has been rejected heretofore. Well. It may, nevertheless, be the true theory. The Copernican astronomy was argued against in a former age and rejected; yet it has prevailed. Newton's law of gravitation was argued against and rejected by a whole generation of philosophers on the continent of Europe; yet it has prevailed. And now all school-boys and girls would call anybody a fool who should deny it. Steam, in all its applications, was argued against and rejected; yet it has prevailed. So the electric telegraph; and, to go back a little, the theory of vaccination,--the circulation of the blood,--a thousand things; yea, Edwards's (the father) theory of virtue, although received by many, has been argued against, and by many rejected; yet it will prevail. Yea, his idea of the unity of the race in Adam was and is argued against and rejected; yet it will prevail. I feel, therefore, no fear that my theory of moral obligation will not be acknowledged because it was argued against and rejected by many in a former age, and may be now. Nay; facts to prove it are accumulating,--facts which were not developed in Edwards's day,--facts showing, irresistibly, that Edwards's theory, which is that most usually now held, is what I say it is,-- _the rejection of revelation, infidelity, and atheism_. The evidence amounts to demonstration.

The question is in a nutshell; it is this:--_Shall man submit to the revealed will of God_, or _to his own will?_ That is the naked question when the fog of confused ideas and unmeaning words is lifted and dispersed.

My position, expressed in the speech delivered in the General Assembly, New York, May, 1856, is this:--"God, in making all things, saw that, in the relations he would constitute between himself and intelligent creatures, and among themselves, NATURAL GOOD AND EVIL would come to pass. In his benevolent wisdom, he then willed LAW to control this good and _evil_; and he thereby made conformity to that law to be _right_, and _non-conformity_ to be wrong. Why? Simply because he saw it to be _good_, and made it to be RIGHT; not because _he saw it to be right_, but because he made it to be right."

Your correspondent replies to this theory in the following words of Edwards:--"Some hold that the foundation of moral obligation is primarily in the will of God. But the will of God is either benevolent or not. If it be benevolent, and on that account the foundation of moral obligation, it is not the source of obligation merely because it is the will of God, but because it is benevolent, and is of a tendency to promote happiness; and this places the foundation of obligation in a tendency to happiness, and not primarily in the will of God. But if the will of God, and that which is the expression of it, the divine law, be allowed to be not benevolent, and are foundation of obligation, we are obliged to conform to them, whatever they be, however malevolent and opposite to holiness and goodness the requirements be. But this, I presume, none will pretend." Very fairly and strongly put; that's to say, if I understand Edwards, he supposes, if God was the devil and man what he is, then man would not be under obligation to obey the devil's will! That's it! Well, I suppose so too; and I reckon most Christians would agree to that statement, Nay, more: I presume nobody ever taught that the mere naked _will_, abstractly considered, if it could be, from the character of God, was the ground of moral obligation? Nay, I think nobody ever imagined that the notion of an infinite Creator presupposes or includes the idea that he is a malevolent Being! I agree, then, with Edwards, that the ultimate ground of obligation is in the fact that God is benevolent, or is a good God. I said that in my speech quoted above. I formally stated that "_God, in his benevolent wisdom, willed law to control the natural good and evil_," &c. What, then, is the point of disagreement between my view and Edwards's? It is in the different ways by which we GET AT the FACT of divine benevolence. I hold that the REVEALED WORD _tells us who God is and what he does_, and is, therefore, the ULTIMATE GROUND OF OBLIGATION. But Edwards holds that HUMAN REASON _must tell us who God is and what he does_, and IS, therefore, the PRIMARY GROUND OF OBEDIENCE. That is my issue with Edwards and others; and it is as broad an issue as _faith in revelation_, or the REJECTION OF IT. I do not charge that Edwards did, or that all who hold with him do, deny the word of God; but I do affirm that their argument does. The matter is plain. For what is revelation? It is that God has appeared in person, and told man in WORD that he is GOD; and told him first in WORD (to be expanded in studying creation and _providence_) that God is a Spirit, eternal, infinite in power, wisdom, goodness, holiness,--the Creator, Preserver, Benefactor. That WORD, moreover, he proved by highest evidence--namely, supernatural evidence--to be _absolute, perfect_ TRUTH as to all FACT affirmed of him and what he does. REVELATION, as claimed in the Bible, was and is THAT THING.

Man, then, having this revelation; is under obligation ever to believe every jot and tittle of that WORD. He at first, no doubt, knew little of the meaning of some facts declared; nay, he may have comprehended nothing of the sense or scope of many facts affirmed. Nay, he may now, after thousands of years, know most imperfectly the meaning of that WORD. But he was and he is, notwithstanding, to believe with absolute faith the WORD,--that God is all he says he is, and does all he says he does,--however that WORD may go beyond his reason, or surprise his feelings, or alarm his conscience, or command his will.

This statement of what revelation is, settles the whole question as presented by Edwards. For REVELATION, as explained, does FIX _forever the foundation of man's moral obligation in the benevolence of God_, PRIMARILY, as it is expressed in the word of God. REVELATION does then, in that sense, FIX obligation in the MERE WILL OF GOD; for, the moment you attempt to establish the foundation _somewhere else_, you have abandoned the ground of revelation. You have left the WILL OF GOD _in his word_, and you have made your rule of right to be the WILL OF MAN in the SELF of the HEART. The proof of what I here say is so plain, even as the writing on the tables of Habakkuk's vision, that he may run that readeth it. Read, then, even as on the tables.

God says in his WORD, "I am all-powerful, all-wise, the Creator." "You may be," says Edwards, "but I want primary foundation for my faith; and I can't take your word for it. I must look first into nature to see if evidence of infinite power and wisdom is there,--to see if evidence of a Creator is there,--and if thou art he!"

Again, God says in his word, "I am benevolent, and my will in my law is expression of that benevolence." "You may tell the truth," Edwards replies, "but I want primary ground for my belief, and I must hold your word suspended until I examine into my reason, my feelings, my conscience, my will,--to see if your WORD harmonizes with my HEART,--to see if what you reveal tends to happiness IN MY NOTION OF HAPPINESS; or tends to right IN MY NOTION OF RIGHT!" That's it. That's the theory of Edwards, Barnes, and others.

And what is this but the attempt to know the divine attributes and character in some other way than through the divine WORD? And what is this but the denial of the divine WORD, except so far as it agrees with the knowledge of the attributes and character of God, obtained in THAT _some other way?_ And what is this but to make the word of God subordinate to the teaching of the HUMAN HEART? And what is this but to make the WILL of God give place to the WILL _of man?_ And what is this but the REJECTION OF REVELATION? Yet this is the result (though not intended by him) of the whole scheme of obligation, maintained by Edwards and by all who agree with him.

Carry it out, and what is the progress and the end of it? This. Human reason--the human heart--will be supreme. Some, I grant, will hold to a revelation of some sort. A thing more and more transcendental,--a thing more and more of fog and moonshine,--fog floating in German cellars from fumes of lager-beer, and moonshine gleaming from the imaginations of the drinkers. Some, like Socrates and Plato, will have a God supreme, personal, glorious, somewhat like the true; and with him many inferior deities,--animating the stars, the earth, mountains, valleys, plains, the sea, rivers, fountains, the air, trees, flowers, and all living things. Some will deny a personal God, and conceive, instead, the intelligent mind of the universe, without love. Some will contend for mere law,--of gravitation and attraction; and some will suggest that all is the result of a fortuitous concourse of atoms! Here, having passed through the shadows and the darkness, we have reached the blackness of infidelity,--blank atheism. No God--yea, all the way the "_fools_" were saying in their hearts, no God. What now is man? Alas! some, the Notts and Gliddons, tell us, man was indeed created millions of ages ago, the Lord only knows when, in swarms like bees to suit the zones of the earth,--while other some, the believers in the _vestiges of creation_, say man is the result of development,--from fire, dust, granite, grass, the creeping thing, bird, fish, four-footed beast, monkey. Yea, and some of these last philosophers are even now going to Africa to try to find men they have heard tell of, who still have tails and are jumping and climbing somewhere in the regions around the undiscovered sources of the Nile.

This is the progress and the result of the Edwards theory; because, deny or hesitate about revelation, and man cannot prove, _absolutely_, any of the things we are considering. Let us see if he can. Edwards writes, "On the supposition that the will or law of God is the primary foundation, reason, and standard of right and virtue, every attempt to prove the moral perfection or attributes of God is absurd." Here, then, Edwards believes, that, to reach the primary foundation of right and virtue, he must not take God's word as to his perfection or attributes, no matter how fully God may have proved his word: no; but he, Edwards, he, man, must first prove them in some other way. And, of course, he believes he can reach such primary foundation by such other proof. Well, let us see how he goes about it. I give him, to try his hand, the easiest attribute,--"POWER." I give him, then, all creation, and providence besides, as his _black-board_, on which to work his demonstration. I give him, then, the lifetime of Methuselah, in which to reach his conclusion of proof.-- Well, I will now suppose we have all lived and waited that long time: what is his proof OF INFINITE POWER? Has he found the EXHIBITION of _infinite power?_ No. He has found proof of GREAT POWER; but he has not reached the DISPLAY of infinite power. What then is his faith in infinite power after such _proof?_ Why, just this: he INFERS _only_, that THE POWER, _which did the things he sees, can go on, and on, and on, to give greater, and greater, and greater manifestations of itself!_ VERY GOOD: _if so be, we can have no better proof_. But that PROOF is infinitely below ABSOLUTE PROOF of infinite power. And all manifestations of power to a _finite creature_, even to the archangel Michael, during countless millions of ages, never gives, because it never can give to him, ABSOLUTE PROOF of infinite power. But the word of GOD gives the PROOF ABSOLUTE, _and in a moment of time!_ "I AM THE ALMIGHTY!" The perfect proof is in THAT WORD OF GOD.

I might set Edwards to work to prove the _infinite wisdom_, the _infinite benevolence_, the _infinite holiness_--yea, the EXISTENCE--of God. And he, finite man, in any examination of creation or providence, must fall infinitely below the PERFECT PROOF.

So then I tell Edwards, and all agreeing with him, that it is absurd to attempt to prove the moral perfection and attributes of God, if he thereby seeks to reach the HIGHEST EVIDENCE, or if he thereby means to find the PRIMARY GROUND of moral obligation.

Do I then teach that man should not seek the proof there is, of the perfection and attributes of God, in _nature and providence_? No. I hold that such proof unfolds the meaning of the FACTS declared in the WORD of God, and is all-important, as such expansion of meaning. But I say, by authority of the Master, that _the highest proof, the absolute proof, the perfect proof_, of the FACTS as to _who God is, and what he does_, and the PRIMARY OBLIGATION _thereupon, is in the_ REVEALED WORD.

FRED. A. ROSS.

Huntsville, Ala., April 3, 1857.

N.B.--In notice of last Witness's extract from Erskine, I remark that Thomas Erskine was, and may yet be, a lawyer of Edinburgh. He wrote _three works_:--one on the _Internal Evidences_, the next on _Faith_, the last on the Freeness of the Gospel. They are all written with great ability, and contain much truth. But all have in them fundamental untruths. There is least in the Evidences; more in the essay on Faith; most in the tract on the Freeness of the Gospel,--which last has been utterly refuted, and has passed away. His Faith is, also, not republished. The Evidences is good, like good men, notwithstanding the evil.

Letters to Rev. A. Barnes.

Introduction.

As part of the great slavery discussion, Rev. A. Barnes, of Philadelphia, published, in October, 1856, a pamphlet, entitled, "The CHURCH and SLAVERY." In this tract he invites every man to utter his views on the subject. And, setting the example, he speaks his own with the greatest freedom and honesty.

In the same freedom of speech, I have considered his views unscriptural, false, fanatical, and infidel. Therefore, while I hold him in the highest respect, esteem, and affection, as a divine and Christian gentleman, and cherish his past relations to me, yet I have in these letters written to him, and of him, just as I would have done had he lived in France or Germany, a stranger to me, and given to the world the refined scoff of the one, or the muddy transcendentalism of the other.

My first letter is merely a glance at some things in his pamphlet, in which I show wherein I agree and disagree with him,--_i.e._ in our estimate of the results of the agitation; in our views of the Declaration of Independence; in our belief of the way men are made infidels; and in our appreciation of the testimonies of past General Assemblies.

The other letters I will notice in similar introductions.

These letters first appeared as original contributions to the Christian Observer, published and edited by Dr. A. Converse, Philadelphia.

I take this occasion to express my regard for him, and my sense of the ability with which he has long maintained the rights and interests of the Presbyterian body, to which we both belong; and the wise and masterly way in which he has vindicated, from the Bible, the truth on the slavery question. To him, too, the public is indebted for the first exhibition of Mr. Barnes's errors in his recent tract which has called forth my reply.

No. I.

Rev. A. Barnes:--

Dear Sir:--You have recently published a tract:--"The Church and Slavery."

"The opinion of each individual," you remark, "contributes to form public sentiment, as the labor of the animalcule in the ocean contributes to the coral reefs that rise above the waves."

True, sir, and beautifully expressed. But while, in harmony with your intimation, I must regard you one of the animalcules, rearing the coral reef of public opinion, I cannot admit your disclaimer of "special influence" among them in their work. Doubtless, sir, you have "special influence,"--and deserve to have. I make no apology for addressing you. I am one of the animalcules.

I agree, and I disagree, with you. I harmonize in your words,--"The present is eminently a time when the views of every man on the subject of slavery should be uttered in unambiguous tones." I agree with you in this affirmation; because the subject has yet to be fully understood; because, when understood, if THE BIBLE does not sanction the system, the MASTER must cease to be the master. The SLAVE must cease to be the slave. He must be _free_, AND EQUAL IN POLITICAL AND SOCIAL LIFE. That is your "_unambiguous tone_". Let it be heard, if that is the word of God.

But if THE BIBLE does sanction the system, then that "unambiguous tone" will silence abolitionists who admit the Scriptures; it will satisfy all good men, and give peace to the country. That is the "_tone_" I want men to hear. Listen to it in the past and present speech of providence. The time was when you had the very public sentiment you are now trying to form. From Maine to Louisiana, the American mind was softly yielding to the impress of emancipation, in some hope, however vague and imaginary. Southern as well as Northern men, in the church and out of it, not having sufficiently studied the word of God, and, under our own and French revolutionary excitement, looking only at the evils of slavery, wished it away from the land. It was a mistaken public sentiment. Yet, such as it was, you had it, and it was doing your work. It was Quaker-like, mild and affectionate. It did not, however, work fast enough for you. You thought that the negro, with his superior attributes of body and mind and higher advantages of the nineteenth century, might reach, in a day, the liberty and equality which the Anglo-American had attained after the struggle of his ancestors during a thousand years! You got up the agitation. You got it up in the Church and State. You got it up over the length and breadth of this whole land. Let me show you some things you have secured, as the results of your work.

First Result of Agitation.

1. The most consistent abolitionists, affirming the sin of slavery, on the maxim of created equality and unalienable right, after torturing the Bible for a while, to make it give the same testimony, felt they could get nothing from the book. They felt that the God of the Bible disregarded the thumb-screw, the boot, and the wheel; that he would not speak for them, but against them. These consistent men have now turned away from the word, in despondency; and are seeking, somewhere, an abolition Bible, an abolition Constitution for the United States, and an abolition God.

This, sir, is the first result of your agitation:--the very van of your attack repulsed, and driven into infidelity.

A Second Result of Agitation.

2. Many others, and you among them, are trying in exactly the same way just mentioned to make the Bible speak against slave-holding. You get nothing by torturing the English version. People understand English. Nay, you get little by applying the rack to the Hebrew and Greek; even before a tribunal of men like you, who proclaim beforehand that Moses, in Hebrew, and Paul, in Greek, must condemn slavery because "it is a violation of the first sentiments of the Declaration of Independence." You find it difficult to persuade men that Moses and Paul were moved by the Holy Ghost to

sanction the philosophy of Thomas Jefferson! You find it hard to make men believe that Moses saw in the mount, and Paul had vision in heaven, that this future apostle of Liberty was inspired by Jesus Christ.

You torture very severely. But the muscles and bones of those old men are tough and strong. They won't yield under your terrible wrenchings. You get only groans and mutterings. You claim these voices, I know, as testimony against slavery. But you cannot torture in secret as in olden times. When putting the question, you have to let men be present,--who tell us that Moses and Paul won't speak for you,--that they are silent, like Christ before Pilate's scourging-men; or, in groans and mutterings,--the voices of their sorrow and the tones of their indignation,--they rebuke your pre-judgment of the Almighty when you say if the Bible sanctions slavery, "it neither ought to be nor could be received by mankind as a divine revelation."

This, sir, is the second result you have gained by your agitation. You have brought a thousand Northern ministers of the gospel, with yourself, to the verge of the same denial of the word of God which they have made, who are only a little ahead of you in the road you are travelling.

A Third Result of Agitation.

3. Meanwhile, many of your most pious men, soundest scholars, and sagacious observers of providence, have been led to study the Bible more faithfully in the light of the times. And they are reading it more and more in harmony with the views which have been reached by the highest Southern minds, to wit:--That the relation of master and slave is sanctioned by the Bible;--that it is a relation belonging to the same category as those of husband and wife, parent and child, master and apprentice, master and hireling;--that the relations of husband and wife, parent and child, _were ordained in Eden for man, as man_, and _modified after the fall_, while the relation of slavery, as a system of labor, is _only one form of the government ordained of God over fallen and degraded man_;--that the evils in the system are the same evils of OPPRESSION we see in the relation of husband and wife,

and all other forms of government;--that slavery, as a relation, suited to the more degraded or the more ignorant and helpless types of a sunken humanity, is, like all government, intended _as the proof of the curse of such degradation, and at the same time to elevate and bless_;--that the relation of husband and wife, being for man, as man, _will ever be over him_, while slavery will remain so long as God sees it best, as a controlling power over the ignorant, the more degraded and helpless;--and that, when he sees it for the good of the country, he will cause it to pass away, if the slave can be elevated to liberty and equality, political and social, with his master, in that country; or out of that country, if such elevation cannot be given therein, but may be realized in some other land: all which result must be left to the unfoldings of the divine will, _in harmony with the Bible_, and not to a newly-discovered dispensation. These facts are vindicated in the Bible and Providence. In the Old Testament, they stare you in the face:--in the family of Abraham,--in his slaves, bought with his money and born in his house,--in Hagar, running away under her mistress's hard dealing with her, and yet sent back, as a fugitive slave, by the angel,--in the law which authorized the Hebrews to hold their brethren as slaves for a time,--in which parents might sell their children into bondage,--in which the heathen were given to the Hebrews as their slaves forever,--in which slaves were considered so much the money of their master, that the master who killed one by an unguarded blow was, under certain circumstances, sufficiently punished in his slave's death, because he thereby lost his money,--in which the difference between _man-stealing_ and _slave-holding_ is, by law, set forth,--in which the runaway from heathen masters may not be restored, because God gave him the benefits of an adopted Hebrew. In the New Testament:--wherein the slavery of Greece and Rome was recognised,--in the obligations laid on master and slave,--in the close connection of this obligation with the duties of husband and wife, parent and child,--in the obligation to return the fugitive slave to his master,--and _in the condemnation of every abolition principle_, "AS DESTITUTE OF THE TRUTH." (1 Tim. vi. 1-5.)

This view of slavery is becoming more and more, not only the settled decision of the Southern but of the best Northern mind, with a movement so strong that you have been startled by it to write the pamphlet now lying before me.

This is the third result you have secured:--to make many of the best men in the North see the infidelity of your philosophy, falsely so called, on the subject of slavery, in the clearer and clearer light of the Scriptures.

Another Result of Agitation.

4. The Southern slave-holder is now satisfied, as never before, that the relation of master and slave is sanctioned by the Bible; and he feels, as never before, the obligations of the word of God. He no longer, in his ignorance of the Scriptures, and afraid of its teachings, will seek to defend his common-sense opinions of slavery by arguments drawn from "Types of Mankind," and other infidel theories; but he will look, in the light of the Bible, on all the good and evil in the system. And when the North, as it will, shall regard him holding from God this high power for great good,--when the North shall no more curse, but bid him God-speed,--then he will bless himself and his slave, in nobler benevolence. With no false ideas of created equality and unalienable right, but with the Bible in his heart and hand, he will do justice and love mercy in higher and higher rule. Every evil will be removed, and the negro will be elevated to the highest attainments he can make, and be prepared for whatever destiny God intends. This, sir, is the fourth result of your agitation:-- to make the Southern master _know_, from the Bible, his right to be a master, and his duty to his slave.

These four results are so fully before you, that I think you must see and feel them. You have brought out, besides, tremendous political consequences, giving astonishing growth and spread to the slave power: on these I cannot dwell. Sir, are you satisfied with these consequences of the agitation you have gotten up? I am. I thank God that the great deep of the American mind has been blown upon by the wind of abolitionism. I rejoice that the stagnant water of that American mind has been so greatly purified. I rejoice that the infidelity and the semi-infidelity so long latent have been set free. I rejoice that the sober sense North and South, so strangely asleep and silent, has risen up to hear the word of God and to speak it to the land. I rejoice that all the South now know that God gives the right to hold slaves, and, with that right, obligations they must fulfil. I rejoice that the day has dawned in which the North and South will think and feel and act together on the subject of slavery. I thank God for the agitation. May he forgive the folly and wickedness of many who have gotten it up! May he reveal more and more, that surely the wrath of man shall praise him, while the remainder of wrath he will restrain!

Declaration of Independence.

I agree with you, sir, that the second paragraph of the Declaration of Independence contains _five affirmations_, declared to be self-evident truths, which, if truths, do sustain you and all abolitionists in every thing you say as to the right of the negro to liberty; and not only to liberty,--to equality, political and social. But I disagree with you as to their truth, and I say that not one of said affirmations is a self-evident truth, or a truth at all. On the contrary, that each one is contrary to the Bible; that each one, separately, is denied; and that all five, collectively, are denied and upset by the Bible, by the natural history of man, and by providence, in every age of the world. I say this now. In a subsequent communication, I will prove what I affirm. For the present I merely add, that the Declaration of Independence stands in no need of these false affirmations. It was, and is, a beautiful whole without them. It was, and is, without these imaginary maxims, the simple statement of the grievances the colonies had borne from the mother-country, and their right _as colonies_, when thus oppressed, to declare themselves independent. That is to say, the right given of God to oppressed children to seek protection in another family, or to set up for themselves somewhat before _twenty-one_ or natural maturity; right belonging to them _in the British family;_ right sanctioned of God; right blessed of God, in the resistance of the colonies _as colonies_--not as individual men--to the attempt of the mother-country to consummate her tyranny. But God gives no sanction to the affirmation that he has _created all men equal_; that this is _self-evident,_ and that he has given them _unalienable rights;_ that he has made government to _derive its power solely from their consent_, and that he has given them the right to change that government in their mere pleasure. All this--every word of it, every jot and tittle--is the liberty and equality claimed by infidelity. God has cursed it seven times in France since 1793; and he will curse it there seventy times seven, if Frenchmen prefer to be pestled so often in Solomon's mortar. He has cursed it in Prussia, Austria, Germany, Italy, Spain. He will curse it as long as time, whether it is affirmed by Jefferson, Paine, Robespierre, Ledru Rollin, Kossuth, Greeley, Garrison, or Barnes.

Sir, that paragraph is an excrescence on the tree of our liberty. I pray you take it away. Worship it if you will, and in a manner imitate the Druid. He gave reverence to the _mistletoe_, but first he removed the parasite from the noble tree. Do you the same. Cut away this mistletoe with golden knife, as did the Druid; enshrine its imaginary divinity in a grove or cave; then retire there, and leave our oak to stand in its glory in the light of heaven. Men have been afraid to say all this for years, just as they have been timid to assert that God has placed master and slave in the same relation as husband and wife. Public sentiment, which you once had and have lost, suppressed this utterance as the other. But now, men speak out; and I, for one, will tell you what the Bible reveals as to that part of the Declaration of Independence, as fearlessly as I tell you what it says of the system of slavery.

How Men are made Infidels.

I agree with you that some men have been, are, and will be, made infidels by hearing that God has ordained slavery as one form of his government over depraved mankind. But how does this fact prove that the Bible does not sanction slavery? Why, sir, you have been all your life teaching that some men are made infidels by hearing any truth of the Bible;--that some men are made infidels by hearing the Trinity, Depravity, Atonement, Divinity of Christ, Resurrection, Eternal Punishment. True: and these men find "_great laws of their nature,--instinctive feelings_"--just such as you find against slavery, and not more perverted in them than in you, condemning all this Bible. And they hold now, with your sanction, that a book affirming such facts "cannot be from God."

Sir, some men are made infidels by hearing the Ten Commandments, and they find "_great laws of their nature_," as strong in them as yours in you against slavery, warring against every one of these commandments. And they declare now, with your authority, that a book imposing such restraints upon human nature, "_cannot be from God_" Sir, what is it makes infidels? You have been wont to answer, "They will not have God to rule over them. They will not have the BIBLE _to control the great laws of their nature."_ Sir, that is the true answer. And you know that the great instinct of liberty is only one of _three great laws_, needing special teaching and government:--that is to say, _the instinct to rule; the instinct to submit to be ruled; and the instinct for liberty._ You know, too, that the instinct to submit is the strongest, the instinct to rule is next, and that the aspiration for liberty is the weakest. Hence you know the overwhelming majority of men have ever been willing to be slaves; masters have been next in number; while the few have struggled for freedom.

The Bible, then, in proclaiming God's will _as to these three great impulses_, will be rejected by men, exactly as they have yielded forbidden control to the one or the other of them. The Bible will make infidels of _masters_, when God calls to them to rule right, or to give up rule, if they have allowed the instinct of power to make them hate God's authority. Pharaoh spoke for all infidel rulers when he said, "_Who is the Lord that I should obey his voice?_"

The Bible will make infidels of _slaves_, when God calls to them to aspire to be free, if they have permitted the instinct of submission to make them hate his commands. The Israelites in the wilderness revealed ten times, in their murmuring, _the slave-instinct_ in all ages:--"_Would to God we had died in the wilderness!_"

You know all this, and you condemn these infidels. Good.

But, sir, you know equally well that the Bible will make infidels of men _affirming the instinct of liberty,_ when God calls them to learn of him how much liberty he gives, and how he gives it, and when he gives it, if they have so yielded to this law of their nature as to make them despise the word of the Lord. Sir, Korah, Dathan, and Abiram spoke out just what the liberty-and-equality men have said in all time:--"_Ye, Moses and Aaron, take too much upon you, seeing all the congregation are holy, every one of them: wherefore, then, lift ye up yourselves above the congregation?"_ Verily, sir, these men were intensely excited by "_the great law of our nature,--the great instinct of freedom."_ Yea, they told God to his face they had looked within, and found the _higher law of liberty and equality--the eternal right--in their intuitional consciousness_; and that they would not submit to his will in the elevation of Moses and Aaron above them.

Verily, sir, you, in the spirit of Korah, now proclaim and say, "Ye masters, and ye white men who are not masters, North and South, ye take too much upon you, seeing the negro is created your equal, and, by unalienable right, is as free as you, and entitled to all your political and social life. Ye take, then, too much upon you in excluding him from your positions of wealth and honor, from your halls of legislation, and from your palace of the nation, and from your splendid couch, and from your fair women with long hair on that couch and in that gilded chariot: wherefore, then, lift ye up yourselves above the negro?"

Verily, sir, Korah, Dathan, and Abiram said all we have ever heard from abolition-platforms or now listen to from you. But the Lord made the earth swallow up Korah, Dathan, and Abiram!

I agree with you then, sir, fully, that some men have been, are, and will be, made infidels by hearing that God, in the Bible, has ordained slavery. But I hold this to be no argument against the fact that the Bible does so teach, because men are made infidels by any other doctrine or precept they hate to believe.

Sir, no man has said all this better than you. And I cannot express my grief that you--in the principle now avowed, _that every man must interpret the Bible as he chooses to reason and feel_--sanction all the infidelity in the world, obliterate your "_Notes_" on the Bible, and deny the preaching of your whole life, so far as God may, in his wrath, permit you to expunge or recall the words of the wisdom of your better day.

Testimonies of General Assemblies.

I agree with you that the Presbyterian Church, both before and since its division, has testified, after a fashion, against slavery. But some of its action has been very curious testimony. I know not how the anti-slavery resolutions of 1818 were gotten up; nor how in some Assemblies since. I can guess, however, from what I do know, as to how such resolutions passed in Buffalo in 1853, and in New York in 1856. I know that in Buffalo they were at first voted down by a large majority. Then they were reconsidered in mere courtesy to men who said they wanted to speak. So the resolutions were passed after some days, in which the screws were applied and turned, in part, _by female hands_, to save the chairman of the committee from the effects of the resolutions being finally voted down!

I know that, in New York, the decision of the Assembly to spread the minority report on the minutes was considered, in the body and out of it, as a Southern victory; for it revealed, however glossed over, that many in the house, who could not vote directly for the minority report, did in fact prefer it to the other.

I was not in Detroit in 1850; but I think it was established in New York last May that that Detroit testimony was so admirably worded that both Southern and Northern men might vote for it with clear consciences!

I need not pursue the investigation. I admit that, after this sort, you have the stultified abstractions of the New School Presbyterian Church,--while I have its common sense; you have its Delphic words,--I have its actions; you have the traditions of the elders making void the word of God,--I have the providence of God restraining the church from destroying itself and our social organization under folly, fanaticism, and infidelity.

You, sir, seem to acknowledge this; for, while you appear pleased with the testimony of the New School Presbyterian Church, such as it is, you lament that the Old School have not been true to the resolutions of 1818,--that, in that branch of the church, it is questionable whether those resolutions could now be adopted. You lament the silence of the Episcopal, the Southern Methodist, and the Baptist denominations; you might add the Cumberland Presbyterian Church. And you know that in New England, in New York, and in the Northwest, many testify against us as a pro-slavery body. You lament that so many members of the church, ministers of the gospel, and editors of religious papers, defend the system; you lament that so large a part of the religious literature of the land, though having its seat North and sustained chiefly by Northern funds, shows a perpetual deference to the slave-holder; you lament that, after fifty years, nothing has been done to arrest slavery; you lament and ask, "Why should this be so?" In saying this, you acknowledge that, while you have been laboring to get and have reached the abstract testimony of the church, all diluted as it is, the common-sense fact has been and is more and more brought out, in the providence of God, that _the slave-power has been and is gaining ground in the United States_. In one word, you have contrived to get, in confused utterance, the voice of the Sanhedrim; while Christ himself has been preaching in the streets of our Jerusalem the true meaning of slavery as one form of his government over fallen men.

These, then, are some of the things I promised to show as the results of your agitation. This is the "_tone_" of the past and present speech of Providence on the subject of slavery. You seem disturbed. I feel sure things are going on well as to that subject. Speak on, then, "in unambiguous tones." But, sir, when you desire to go from words to actions,--when you intimate that the constitution of the Presbyterian Church may be altered to permit such action, or that, without its alteration, the church can detach itself from slavery by its existing laws or the modification of them,--then I understand you to mean that you desire to deal, in fact, with slave-holders as offenders. Then, sir, _you mean to exscind the South_; for it is absurd to imagine that you suppose the South will submit to such action. You mean, then, to _exscind the South, or to exscind yourself and others_, or to compel the South to withdraw. Your tract, just published, is, I suppose, intended by you to prepare the next General Assembly for such movement? What then? Will you make your "American Presbyterian," and your Presbyterian House, effect that great change in the religious literature of the land whereby the subject of slave-holding shall be approached precisely as you deal with "theft, highway-robbery, or piracy?" Will you, then, by act of Assembly, Synod, Presbytery, Session, deny your pulpits, and communion-bread and wine, to slave-holding ministers, elders, and members? Will you, then, tell New England, and especially little Rhoda, We have purified our skirts from the blood: forgive us, and take us again to your love? What then? Will you then ostracize the South and compel the abolition of slavery? Sir, do you bid us fear these coming events, thus casting their shadow before from the leaves of your book?

Sir, you may destroy the integrity of the New School Presbyterian Church. So much evil you may do; but you will hereby only add immensely to the great power and good of the Old School; and you will make disclosures of Providence, unfolding a consummation of things very different from the end you wish to accomplish for your country and the world.

I write as one of the animalcules contributing to the coral reef of public opinion.

F. A. Ross.

No. II.

Government Over Man a Divine Institute.

This letter is the examination and refutation of the infidel theory of human government foisted into the Declaration of Independence.

I had written this criticism in different form for publication, before Mr. Barnes's had appeared. I wrote it to vindicate my affirmation in the General Assembly which met in New York, May last, on this part of the Declaration. My views were maturely formed, after years of reflection, and weeks--nay months--of carefully-penned writing.

And thus these truths, from the Bible, Providence, and common sense, were like rich freight, in goodly ship, waiting for the wind to sail; when lo, Mr. Barnes's abolition-breath filled the canvas, and carried it out of port into the wide, the free, the open sea of American public thought. There it sails. If pirate or other hostile craft comes alongside, the good ship has guns.

I ask that this paper be carefully read more than once, twice, or three times. Mr. Barnes, I presume, will not so read it. He is committed. Greeley may notice it with his sparkling wit, albeit he has too much sense to grapple with its argument. The Evangelist-man will say of it, what he would say if Christ were casting out devils in New York,--"He casteth out devils through Beelzebub the chief of the devils." Yea, this Evangelist-man says that my version of the golden rule is "diabolical;" when truly that version is the word of the Spirit, as Christ's casting out devils was the work of the Holy Ghost.

Gerrett Smith, Garrison, Giddings, do already agree with me, that they are right if Jefferson spoke the truth. Yea, whether the Bible be true, is no question with them no more than with him. Yea, they hold, as he did, that whether there be one God or twenty, it matters not: the fact either way, in men's minds, neither breaks the leg nor picks the pocket. (See Jefferson's Notes on Virginia.) Messrs. Beecher and Cheever will find nothing in me to aid them in speaking to the mobs of Ephesus and Antioch. They are making shrines, and crying, Great is Diana. Mrs. Stowe is on the Dismal Swamp, with Dred for her Charon, to paddle her light canoe, by the fire-fly lamps, to the Limbo of Vanity, of which she is the queen. None of these will read with attention or honesty, if at all, this examination of what Randolph long ago said was a fanfaronade of nonsense. These are all wiser "than seven men that can render a reason."

But there are thousands, North and South, who will read this refutation, and will feel and acknowledge that in the light of God's truth the notion of created equality and unalienable right is falsehood and infidelity.

Rev. A. Barnes:--

Dear Sir:--In my first letter I promised to prove that the paragraph in the Declaration of Independence, which contains the affirmation of created equality and unalienable rights, has no sanction from the word of God. I now meet my obligation.

The time has come when civil liberty, as revealed in the Bible and in Providence, must be re-examined, understood, and defended against infidel theories of human rights. The slavery question has brought on this conflict; and, strange as it may seem, the South, the land of the slave, is summoned by God to defend the liberty he gives; while the North, the clime of the free, misunderstands and changes the truth of God into a lie,--claiming a liberty he does not give. Wherefore is this? I reply:---

God, when he ordained government over men, gave to the individual man RIGHTS, only as he is under government. He first established the family; hence all other rule is merely the family expanded. The good of the family limited the rights of every member. God required the family, and then the state, so to rule as to give to every member the good which is his, in harmony with the welfare of the whole; and he commanded the individual to seek _that good_, and NO MORE.

Now, mankind being depraved, government has ever violated its obligation to rule for the benefit of the entire community, and has wielded its power in oppression. Consequently, the governed have ever struggled to secure the good which was their right. But, in this struggle, they have ever been tempted to go beyond the limitation God had made, and to seek supposed good, not given, in rights, prompted by _self-will_, destructive of the state.

Government thus ever existing in oppression, and people thus ever rising up against despotism, have been the history of mankind.

The Reformation was one of the many convulsions in this long-continued conflict. In its first movements, men claimed the liberty the Bible grants. Soon they ran into licentiousness. God then stayed the further progress of emancipation in Europe, because the spread of the asserted liberty would have made infidelity prevail over that part of the continent where the Reformation was arrested. God preferred Romanism, and other despotisms, modified as they were by the struggle, to rule for a time, than have those countries destroyed under the sway of a licentious freedom.

In this contest the North American colonies had their rise, and they continued the strife with England until they declared themselves independent.

That "Declaration" affirmed not only the liberty sanctioned of the Bible, but also the liberty constituting infidelity. Its first paragraph, to the word "_separation_," is a noble introduction. Omit, then, what follows, to the sentence beginning "_Prudence will dictate_," and the paper, thus expurgated, is complete, and is then simply the complaint of the colonies against the government of England, which had oppressed them beyond further submission, and the assertion of their right to be free and independent States.

This declaration was, in that form, nothing more than the affirmation of the right God gives to children, in a family, applied to the colonies, in regard to their mother-country. That is to say, children have, from God, RIGHT, AS CHILDREN, when cruelly treated, to secure the good to which they are entitled, as children, IN THE FAMILY. They may secure this good by becoming part of another family, or by setting up for themselves, if old enough. So the colonies had, from God, right as colonies, when oppressed beyond endurance, to exchange the British family for another, or, if of sufficient age, to establish their own household. The Declaration, then, in that complaint of oppression and affirmation of right, in the colonies, to be independent, asserts liberty sanctioned by the word of God. And therefore the pledge to that Declaration, of "lives, fortune, and sacred honor," was blessed of Heaven, in the triumph of their cause.

But the Declaration, in the part I have omitted, affirms other things, and very different. It asserts facts and rights as appertaining to man, not in the Scriptures, but contrary thereto. Here is the passage:--

"We hold these truths to be self-evident,--that all men are created equal; that they are endowed by their Creator with certain unalienable rights; that among these are life, liberty, and the pursuit of happiness. That to secure these rights, governments are instituted among men, deriving their just powers from the consent of the governed; that whenever any form of government becomes destructive of these ends, it is the right of the people to alter or abolish it, and to institute a new government, laying its foundation on such principles, and organizing its powers in such form, as to them shall seem most likely to effect their safety and happiness."

This is the affirmation of the liberty claimed by infidelity. It teaches as a fact that which is not true; and it claims as right that which God has not given. It asserts nothing new, however. It lays claim to that individual right beyond the limitation God has put, which man has ever asserted when in his struggle for liberty he has refused to be guided and controlled by the word and providence of his Creator.

The paragraph is a chain of four links, each of which is claimed to be a self-evident truth.

The first and controlling assertion is, "that ALL MEN ARE CREATED EQUAL;" which proposition, as I understand it, is, that every man and woman on earth is created with equal attributes of body and mind.

Secondly, and consequently, that every individual has, by virtue of his or her being created the equal of each and every other individual, the right to life, liberty, and the pursuit of happiness, so in his or her own keeping that that right is unalienable without his or her consent.

Thirdly, it follows, that government among men must derive its just powers only from the consent of the governed; and, as the governed are the aggregate of individuals, then each person must consent to be thus controlled before he or she can be rightfully under such authority.

Fourthly, and finally, that whenever any form of government becomes destructive of the right to life, liberty, and the pursuit of happiness, _as each such individual man or woman may think_, then each such person may rightly set to work to alter or abolish such form, and institute a new government, on such principles and in such form as to them shall seem most likely to effect their safety and happiness.

This is the celebrated averment of created equality, and unalienable right to life, liberty, and pursuit of happiness, with the necessary consequences. I have fairly expanded its meaning. It is the old infidel averment. It is not true in any one of its assertions.

All Men not created equal.

It is not a truth, _self-evident,_ that all men are created equal. Webster, in his dictionary, defines "Self-evident--Evident without proof or reason: clear conviction upon a bare presentation to the mind, as that two and three make five."

Now, I affirm, and you, I think, will not contradict me, that the position, "_all men are created equal"_ is not self-evident; that the nature of the case makes it impossible for it to be self-evident. For the created nature of man is not in the class of things of which such self-evident propositions can by possibility be predicated. It is equally clear and beyond debate, that it is not _self-evident_ that all men have _unalienable rights_, that governments derive their just powers from the consent of the governed, and may be altered or abolished whenever to them such rights may be better secured. All these assertions can be known to be true or false only from revelation of the Creator, or from examination and induction of reasoning, covering the nature and the obligations of the race on the whole face of the earth. What revelation and examination of facts do teach, I will now show. The whole battle-ground, as to the truth of this series of averments, is on the first affirmation, "that all men are created equal." Or, to keep up my first figure, the strength of the chain of asserted truths depend on that first link. It must then stand the following perfect trial.

God reveals to us that he created man in his image, _i.e._ a spirit endowed with attributes resembling his own,--to reason, to form rule of right, to manifest various emotions, to will, to act,--and that he gave him a body suited to such a spirit, (Gen. i. 26, 27, 28;) that he created MAN "_male and female_," (Gen. i. 27;) that he made the woman "_out of the man_," (Gen. ii. 23;) that he made "_the man the image and glory of God_, but the woman the glory of the man. For the man is not of the woman, but the woman of the man. Neither was the man _created for the woman_, but the woman _for the man_," (1 Cor. xi.;) that he made the woman to be the weaker vessel, (1 Pet. iii. 7.) Here, then, God created the race to be in the beginning TWO,--a male and a female MAN; one of them not equal to the other _in attributes of body and mind_, and, as we shall see presently, not equal in rights as to government. Observe, this inequality was fact as to the TWO, in the perfect state wherein they were created.

But these two fell from that perfect state, became depraved, and began to be degraded in body and mind. This statement of the original inequality in which man was created controls all that comes after, in God's providence and in the natural history of the race.

Providence, in its comprehensive teaching, "says that God, soon after the flood, subjected the races to all the influences of the different zones of the earth;"--"That he hath made of one blood all nations of men for to dwell on all the face of the earth, and hath determined the times before appointed and the bounds of their habitation; that they should seek the Lord if haply they might feel after him and find him, though he be not far from every one of us." (Acts xvii. 26, 27.)

These "bounds of their habitation" have had much to do in the natural history of man; for "_all men_" have been "_created_," or, more correctly, _born_, (since the race was "created" once only at the first,) with attributes of body and mind derived from the TWO unequal parents, and these attributes, in every individual, the combined result of the parental natures. "_All men_," then, come into the world under influences upon the amalgamated and transmitted body and mind, from depravity and degradation, sent down during all the generations past; and, therefore, under causes of inequality, acting on each individual from climate, from scenery, from food, from health, from sickness, from love, from hatred, from government, inconceivable in variety and power. Under such causes, to produce infinite shades of inequality, physical and mental, in birth--if "all men" were created equal (_i.e._ born equal) in attributes of body and mind--such "creation" would be a violation of all the known analogies in the world of life.

Do, then, the facts in man's natural history exhibit this departure from the laws of life and spirit? Do they prove that "all men are created equal"? Do they show that every man and every woman of Africa, Asia, Europe, America, and the islands of the seas, is created each one equal in body and mind to each other man or woman on the face of the earth, and that this has always been?

Need I extend these questions? Methinks, sir, I hear you say, what others have told me, that the "Declaration" is not to be understood as affirming what is so clearly false, but merely asserts that all men are "created equal" in _natural rights._

I reply that that is not the meaning of the clause before us; for that is the meaning of the next sentence,--the second in the series we are considering.

There are, as I have said, four links to the chain of thought in this passage:--1. That all men are created equal. 2. That they are endowed by the Creator with certain unalienable rights. 3. That government derives its just powers from the consent of the governed. 4. That the people may alter and abolish it, &c.

These links are logical sequences. All men--man and woman--are created equal,--equal in _attributes of body and mind_; (for that is the only sense in which they could be created equal;) therefore they are endowed with right to life, liberty, and pursuit of happiness, unalienable, except in their consent; consequently such consent is essential to all rightful government; and, finally and _irresistibly_, the people have supreme right to alter or abolish it, &c.

The meaning, then, I give to that first link, and to the chain following, is the sense, because, if you deny that meaning to the _first link_, then the others have no logical truth whatever. Thus:--

If all men are not created equal in attributes of body and mind, then the inequality may be so great that such men cannot be endowed with right to life, liberty, and pursuit of happiness, unalienable save in their _consent_; then government over such men cannot rightfully rest upon their _consent_; nor can they have right to alter or abolish government in their mere determination.

Yea, sir, you concede every thing if you admit that the "Declaration" does not mean to affirm that all men are "_created_" equal in body and mind.

I will suppose in the Alps a community of Cretins,--_i.e._ deformed and helpless idiots,--but among them many from the same parents, who, in body and mind, by birth are comparatively Napoleons. Now, this _inequality_, physical and mental, by birth, makes it impossible that the government over these Cretins can be in their "consent." The Napoleons must rule. The

Napoleons must absolutely control their "life, liberty, and pursuit of happiness," for the good of the community. Do you reply that I have taken an extreme case? that everybody admits sensible people must govern natural fools? Ay, sir, there is the rub. _Natural fools_! Are some men, then, "_created_" natural fools? Very well. Then you also admit that some men are created just a degree above natural fools!--and, consequently, that men are "_created_" in all degrees, gradually rising in the scale of intelligence. Are they not "_created_" just above the brute, with savage natures along with mental imbecility and physical degradation? Must the Napoleons govern the Cretins without their "consent"? Must they not also govern without their "consent" these types of mankind, whether one, two, three, thirty, or three hundred degrees above the Cretins, if they are still greatly inferior by nature? Suppose the Cretins removed from the imagined community, and a colony of Australian ant-catchers or California lizard-eaters be in their stead: must not the Napoleons govern these? And, if you admit inequality to be in birth, then that inequality is the very ground of the reason why the Napoleons must govern the ant-catchers and lizard-eaters. Remove these, and put in their place an importation of African negroes. Do you admit their inferiority by "CREATION?" Then the same control over them must be the irresistible fact in common sense and Scripture of God. The Napoleons must govern. They must govern without asking "consent,"--if the inequality be such that "_consent_" would be evil, and not good, in the family--the state.

Yea, sir, if you deny that the "Declaration" asserts "all men are created equal" in body and mind, then you admit the inequality may be such as to make it impossible that in such cases men have rights unalienable save in their "consent;" and you admit it to be impossible that government in such circumstances can exist in such "_consent_." But, if you affirm the "Declaration" does mean that men are "created equal" in attributes of body and mind, then you hold to an equality which God, in his word, and providence, and the natural history of man, denies to be truth.

I think I have fairly shown, from Scripture and facts, that the first averment is not the truth; and have reduced it to an absurdity. I will now regard the second, third, and fourth links of the chain.

I know they are already broken; for, the whole chain being but an electric current from a vicious imagination, I have destroyed the whole by breaking the first link. Or was it but a cluster from a poisonous vine, then I have killed the branches by cutting the vine. I will, however, expose the other three sequences by a distinct argument covering them all.

Authority Delegated to Adam.

God gave to Adam sovereignty over the human race, in his first decree:--"He shall rule over thee." That was THE INSTITUTION OF GOVERNMENT. It was not based on the "_consent_" of Eve, the governed. It was from God. He gave to Adam like authority to rule his children. It was not derived from their "_consent_". It was from God. He gave Noah the same sovereignty, with express power over life, liberty, and pursuit of happiness. It was not founded in "_consent_" of Shem, Ham, and Japheth, and their wives. It was from God. He then determined the habitations of men on all the face of the earth, and indicated to them, in every clime, the form and power of their governments. He gave, directly, government to Israel. He just as truly gave it to Idumea, to Egypt, and to Babylon, to the Arab, to the Esquimaux, the Caffre, the Hottentot, and the negro.

God, in the Bible, decides the matter. He says, "Let every soul be subject unto the higher powers. For there is no power but of God: the powers that be are ordained of God. Whosoever therefore resisteth the power, resisteth the ordinance of God: and they that resist shall receive to themselves damnation. For rulers are not a terror to good works, but to the evil. Wilt thou then not be afraid of the power? Do that which is good, and thou shalt have praise of the same: for he is the minister of God to thee for good. But if thou do that which is evil, be afraid, for he beareth not the sword in vain: for he is the minister of God, a revenger to execute wrath upon him that doeth evil. Wherefore ye must needs be subject, not only for wrath, but also for conscience' sake. For this cause pay ye tribute also: for they are God's ministers, attending continually upon this very thing. Render, therefore, to all their dues; tribute to whom tribute is due; custom to whom custom; fear to whom fear; honor to whom honor." (Rom. xiii. 1-7.)

Here God reveals to us that he has delegated to government his own RIGHT _over life, liberty, and pursuit of happiness_; and that that RIGHT is not, in any sense, from the "_consent_" of the governed, but is directly from him. Government over men, whether in the family or in the state, is, then, as directly from God as it would be if he, in visible person, ruled in the family or in the state. I speak not only of the RIGHT simply to govern, but the mode of the government, and the extent of the power. Government can do ALL which God _would do,--just_ THAT,--_no more, no less_. And it is bound to do just THAT,--_no more, no less_. Government is responsible to God, if it fails to do just THAT which He himself would do. It is under responsibility, then, to rule in righteousness. It must not oppress. It must give to every individual "_life, liberty, and pursuit of happiness_," in harmony with the good of the family,--the state,--_as God himself would give it_,--just THAT, _no more, no less_.

This passage of Scripture settles the question, From whence has government RIGHT to rule, and what is the extent of its power? The RIGHT is from God, and the EXTENT of the power is just THAT to which God would exercise it if he were personally on the earth. God, in this passage, and others, settles, with equal clearness, from whence is the OBLIGATION to submit to government, and what is the extent of the duty of obedience? The OBLIGATION to submit is not from individual RIGHT to consent or not to consent to government,--but the OBLIGATION to submit is directly from God.

The EXTENT of the duty of obedience is equally revealed--in this wise: so long as the government rules in righteousness, the duty is perfect obedience. So soon, however, as government requires that which God, in his word, _forbids the subject to do_, he must obey God, and not man. He must refuse to obey man. But, inasmuch as the obligation to submit to authority of government is so great, the subject must know it is the will of God, that he shall refuse to obey, before he assumes the responsibility of resistance to the powers that be. His conscience will not justify him before God, if he mistakes his duty. He may be all the more to blame for having SUCH A CONSCIENCE. Let him, then, be CERTAIN he can say, like Peter and John, "Whether it be right, in the sight of God, to hearken unto you more than unto God, judge ye."

But, when government requires that which God does not forbid the subject to do, although in that the government may have transcended the line of its righteous rule, the subject must, nevertheless, submit,--until oppression has gone to the point at which God makes RESISTANCE _to be duty._ And that point is when RESISTANCE will clearly be _less of evil, and more of good_, TO THE COMMUNITY, than further submission.

That is the rule of duty God gives to the whole people, or to the _minority_, or to the _individual_, to guide them in resistance to the powers that be.

It is irresistibly certain that He who ordains government _has, alone, the right to alter or abolish it_,--that He who institutes the powers that be has, alone, the right to say when and how the people, in whole or in part, may resist. So, then, the people, in whole, or in part, have no right to resist, to alter, or abolish government, simply because they may deem it destructive of the end for which it was instituted; but they may resist, alter, or abolish, when it shall be seen that God so regards it. This places the great fact where it must be placed,--under the CONTROL of the BIBLE and PROVIDENCE.

Illustrations.

I will conclude with one or two illustrations. God, in his providence, ordains the Russian form of government,--_i.e._ He places the sovereignty in one man, because He sees that such government can secure, for a time, more good to that degraded people than any other form. Now, I ask, Has the emperor _right_, from God, to change at once, in his mere "_consent_," the form of his government to that of the United States? No. God forbids him. Why? Because he would thereby destroy the good, and bring immense evil in his empire. I ask again, Have the Russian serfs and nobles,--yea, all,--"consenting," the right, from God, to make that change? No. For the government of the United States is not suited to them. And, in such an attempt, they would deprive themselves of the blessings they now have, and bring all the horrors of anarchy.

Do you ask if I then hold, that God ordains the Russian type of rule to be perpetual over that people? No. The emperor is bound to secure all of "_life, liberty, and pursuit of happiness_," to each individual, consistent with the good of the nation. And he is to learn his obligation from the Bible, and faithfully apply it to the condition of his subjects. _He will thus gradually elevate them_; while they, on their part, are bound to strive for this elevation, in all the ways in which God may show them the good, and the right, which, more and more, will belong to them in their upward progress. The result of such government and such obedience would be that of a father's faithful training, and children's corresponding obedience. The Russian people would thus have, gradually, that measure of liberty they could bear, under the one-man power,--and then, in other forms, as they might be qualified to realize them. This development would be without convulsion,--as the parent gives place, while the children are passing from the lower to their higher life. It would be the exemplification of Carlyle's illustration of the snake. He says, A people should change their government only as a snake sheds his skin: the new skin is gradually formed under the old one,--and then the snake wriggles out, with just a drop of blood here and there, where the old jacket held on rather tightly.

God ordains the government of the United States. And He places the sovereignty in the will of the majority, because He has trained the people, through many generations in modes of government, to such an elevation in moral and religious intelligence, that such sovereignty is best suited to confer on them the highest right, as yet, to "life, liberty, and the pursuit of happiness." But God requires that that will of the majority be in perfect submission to Him. Once more then I inquire,--Whether the people of this country, yea all of them consenting, have right from God, to abolish now, at this time, our free institutions, and set up the sway of Russia? No. But why? There is one answer only. He tells us that our happiness is in this form of government, and in it, its developed results.

The "Social Compact" not recognised in the Divine Institute_.

Here I pause. So, then, God gives no sanction to the notion of a SOCIAL COMPACT. He never gave to man individual, isolated, natural rights, unalienably in his keeping. He never made him a Caspar Hauser, in the forest, without name or home,--a Melchisedek, in the wilderness, without father, without mother, without descent,--a Robinson Crusoe, on his island, in skins and barefooted, waiting, among goats and parrots, the coming of the canoes and the savages, to enable him to "_consent_" if he would, to the relations of social life.

And, therefore, those five sentences in that second paragraph of the Declaration of Independence are not the truth; so, then, it is not _self-evident_ truth that all men are created equal. So, then, it is not the truth, in fact, that they are created equal. So, then, it is not the truth that God has endowed all men with unalienable right to life, liberty, and pursuit of happiness. So, then, it is not the truth that governments derive their just powers from the consent of the governed. So, then, it is not the truth that the people have right to alter or abolish their government, and institute a new form, whenever to them it shall seem likely to effect their safety and happiness.

The manner in which these unscriptural dogmas have been modified or developed in the United States, I will examine in another paper.

I merely add, that the opinions of revered ancestors, on these questions of right and their application to American slavery, must now, as never before, be brought to the test of the light of the Bible. F.A. Ross.

Huntsville, Ala., Jan. 1857.

Man-Stealing.

This argument on the abolition charge, against the slave-holder,--that he is a man-stealer,--covers the whole question of slavery, especially as it is seen in the Old Testament. The headings in the letter make the subject sufficiently clear.

No. III.

Rev. Albert Barnes:--

Dear Sir:--In my first letter, I merely touched some points in your tract, intending to notice them more fully in subsequent communications. I have, in my second paper, sufficiently examined the imaginary maxims of created equality and unalienable rights.

In this, I will test your views by Scripture more directly. "To the law and to the testimony: if they speak not according to this word, it is because there is no light in them." (Isaiah viii. 20).

The abolitionist charges the slave-holder with being a _man-stealer_. He makes this allegation in two affirmations. First, that the slave-holder is thus guilty, because, the negro having been kidnapped in Africa, therefore those who now hold him, or his children, in bondage, lie under the guilt of that first act. Secondly, that the slave-holder, by the very fact that he is such, is guilty of stealing from the negro his unalienable right to freedom.

This is the charge. It covers the whole subject. I will meet it in all its parts.

The Difference between Man-Stealing and Slave-Holding, as set forth in the Bible_.

The Bible reads thus: (Exodus xxi. 16:)--"He that stealeth a man and selleth him, or if he be found in his hand, he shall surely be put to death."

What, then, is it to kidnap or steal a man? Webster informs us--To kidnap is "to steal a human being, a man, woman, or child; or to seize and forcibly carry away any person whatever, from his own country or state into another." The idea of "_seizing and forcibly carrying away"_ enters into the meaning of the word in all the definitions of law.

The crime, then, set forth in the Bible was not selling a man: but selling a stolen man. The crime was not having a man _in his hand as a slave_; but......in his hand, as a slave, a stolen man. And hence, the penalty of death was affixed, not to selling, buying, or holding man, as a slave, but to the specific offence of _stealing and selling, or holding_ a man _thus stolen, contrary to this law_. Yea, it was _this law_, and this law _only_, which made it wrong. For, under some circumstances, God sanctioned the seizing and forcibly carrying away a man, woman, or child from country or state, into slavery or other condition. He sanctioned the utter destruction of every male and every married woman, and child, of Jabez-Gilead, and the seizure, and forcibly carrying away, four hundred virgins, unto the camp to Shiloh, and there, being given as wives to the remnant of the slaughtered tribe of Benjamin, in the rock Rimmon. Sir, how did that destruction of Jabez-Gilead, and the kidnapping of those young women, differ from the razing of an African village, and forcibly seizing, and carrying away, those not put to the sword? The difference is in this:--God commanded the Israelites to seize and bear off those young women. But he forbids the slaver to kidnap the African. Therefore, the Israelites did right; therefore, the trader does wrong. The Israelites, it seems, gave wives, in that way, to the spared Benjamites, because they had sworn not to give their daughters. But there were six hundred of these Benjamites. Two hundred were therefore still without wives. What was done for them? Why, God authorized the elders of the congregation to tell the two hundred Benjamites to catch every man his wife, of the daughters of Shiloh, when they came out to dance, in the feast of the Lord, on the north side of Bethel. And the children of Benjamin did so, and took them wives, "whom they caught:" (Judges xxi.) God made it right for those Benjamites to catch every man his wife, of the daughters of Shiloh. But he makes it wrong for the trader to catch his slaves of the sons or daughters of Africa. Lest you should try to deny that God authorized this act of the children of Israel, although I believe he did order it, let me remind you of another such case, the authority for which you will not question.

Moses, by direct command from God, destroyed the Midianites. He slew all the males, and carried away all the women and children. He then had all the married women and male children killed; but all the virgins, thirty-two thousand, were divided as spoil among the people. And _thirty-two_ of these virgins, _the Lord's tribute_, were given unto Eleazar, the priest, "as the Lord commanded Moses." (Numbers xxxi.)

Sir, Thomas Paine rejected the Bible on this fact among his other objections. Yea, his reason, his sensibilities, his great law of humanity, his intuitional and eternal sense of right, made it impossible for him to honor such a God. And, sir, on your now avowed principles of interpretation, which are those of Paine, you sustain him in his rejection of the books of Moses and all the word of God.

God's command made it right for Moses to destroy the Midianites and make slaves of their daughters; and I have dwelt upon these facts, to reiterate what I hold to be THE FIRST TRUTH IN MORALS:--that a thing is right, not because it is ever so _per se_, but because God _makes it right_; and, of course, a thing is wrong, not because it is so in the nature of things, but because God makes it wrong. I distinctly have taken, and do take, that ground in its widest sense, and am prepared to maintain it against all comers. He made it right for the sons of Adam to marry their sisters. He made it right for Abraham to marry his half-sister. He made it right for the patriarchs, and David and Solomon, to have more wives than one. He made it right when he gave command to kill whole nations, sparing none. He made it right when he ordered that nations, or such part as he pleased, should be spared and enslaved. He made it right that the patriarchs and the Israelites should hold slaves in harmony with the system of servile labor which had long been in the world. He merely modified that system to suit his views of good among his people. So, then, when he saw fit, they might capture men. So, then, when he forbade the individual Israelite to steal a man, he made it crime, and the penalty death. So, then, that crime was not the mere stealing a man, nor the selling a man, nor the holding a man,--but the _stealing and selling_, or _holding_, a man under circumstances thus forbidden of God.

Was the Israelite Master a Man-Stealer?_

I now ask, Did God intend to make man-stealing and slave-holding the same thing? Let us see. In that very chapter of Exodus (xxi.) which contains the law against man-stealing, and only four verses further on, God says, "If a man smite his servant or his maid with a rod, and he die under his hand, he shall be surely punished: notwithstanding, if he continue a day or two he shall not be punished; for he is his money." (Verses 20, 21.)

Sir, that man was not a hired servant. He was bought with money. He was regarded by God as the money of his master. He was his slave, in the full meaning of a slave, then, and now, bought with money. God, then, did not intend the Israelites to understand, and not one of them ever understood, from that day to this, that Jehovah in his law to Moses regarded the slave-holder as a man-stealer. Man-stealing was a specific offence, with its specific penalty. Slave-holding was one form of God's righteous government over men,--a government he ordained, with various modifications, among the Hebrews themselves, and with sterner features in its relation to heathen slaves.

In Exodus xxi. and Leviticus xxv., various gradations of servitude were enacted, with a careful particularity which need not be misunderstood. Among these, a Hebrew man might be a slave for six years, and then go free with his wife, if he were married when he came into the relation; but if his master had given him a wife, and she had borne him sons or daughters, the wife and her children should be her master's, and he should go out by himself. That is, the man by the law became free, while his wife and children remained slaves. If the servant, however, plainly said, "I love my master, my wife, and my children; I will not go out free: then his master brought him unto the judges, also unto the doorpost, and his master bored his ear through with an awl, and he served him forever." (Ex. xxi. 1-6.) Sir, you have urged discussion:--give us then your views of that passage. Tell us how that man was separated from his wife and children according to the eternal right. Tell us what was the condition of the woman in case the man chose to "go out" without her? Tell us if the Hebrew who thus had his ear bored by his master with an awl was not a slave for life? Tell us, lastly, whether those children were not slaves? And, while on that chapter, tell us whether in the next verses, 7-11, God did not allow the Israelite father to sell his own daughter into bondage and into polygamy by the same act of sale?

I will not dwell longer on these milder forms of slavery, but read to you the clear and unmistakable command of the Lord in Leviticus xxv. 44, 46:--"Both thy bondmen and thy bondmaids which thou shalt have, shall be of the heathen that are round about you; of them shall ye buy bondmen and bondmaids. Moreover, of the children of the strangers that do sojourn among you, of them shall ye buy, and of their families that are with you, which they beget in your land: and they shall be your possession: and ye shall take them for an inheritance for your children after you, to inherit them for a possession; and they shall be your bondmen forever."

Sir, the sun will grow dim with age before that Scripture can be tortured to mean any thing else than just what it says; that God commanded the Israelites to be slave-holders in the strict and true sense over the heathen, in manner and form therein set forth. Do you tell the world that this cannot be the sense of the Bible, because it is "a violation of the first principles of the American Declaration of Independence;" because it grates upon your "instinct of liberty;" because it reveals God in opposition to the "spirit of the age;" because, if it be the sense of the passage, then "the Bible neither ought to be, nor can be, received by mankind as a divine revelation"? That is what you say: that is what Albert Barnes affirms in his philosophy. But what if God in his word says, "Both thy bondmen and thy bondmaids which thou shalt have shall be of the heathen that are round about you"? What if we may then choose between Albert Barnes's philosophy and God's truth?

Or will you say, God, under the circumstances, permitted the Israelites to sin in the matter of slave-holding, just as he permitted them to sin by living in polygamy. Permitted them _to sin!_ No, sir; God commanded them to be slave-holders. He made it the law of their social state. He made it one form of his ordained government among them. Moreover, you take it for granted all too soon, that the Israelites committed sin in their polygamy. God sanctioned their polygamy. It was therefore not sin in them. It was right. But God now forbids polygamy, under the gospel; and now it is sin.

Or will you tell us the iniquity of the Canaanites was then full, and God's time to punish them had come? True; but the same question comes up:--Did God punish the Canaanites by placing them in the relation of slaves to his people, by express command, which compelled them to sin? That's the point. I will not permit you to evade it. In plainer words:--Did God command the Hebrews to make slaves of their fellow-men, to buy them and sell them, to regard them as their money? He did. Then, did the Hebrews sin when they obeyed God's command? No. Then they did what was right, and it was right because God made it so. Then _the Hebrew slave-holder was not a man-stealer_. But, you say, the Southern slave-holder is. Well, we shall see presently.

Just here, the abolitionist who professes to respect the Scriptures is wont to tell us that the whole subject of bondage among the Israelites was so peculiar to God's ancient dispensation, that no analogy between that bondage and Southern slavery can be brought up. Thus he attempts to raise a dust out of the Jewish institutions, to prevent people from seeing that slaveholding then was the same thing that it is now. But, to sustain my interpretation of the plain Scriptures given, I will go back five hundred years before the existence of the Hebrew nation.

I read at that time, (Gen. xiv. 14:)--"And when Abraham heard that his brother was taken captive, he armed his trained servants, born in his own house, three hundred and eighteen, and pursued them even unto Damascus," &c. (Gen. xvii. 27:)--"And all the men of his house, born, in the house, and bought with the money of the stranger, were circumcised." (Gen. xx. 14:)--"And Abimelech took sheep and oxen, and men-servants and women-servants, and gave them unto Abraham." (Gen. xxiv. 34, 35:)--"And he said, I am Abraham's servant; and the Lord hath blessed my master greatly, and he is become great; and he hath given him flocks and herds, and silver and gold, and men-servants and maid-servants, and camels and asses."

Was Abraham a Man-Stealer?_

Sir, what is the common sense of these Scriptures? Why, that the slave-trade existed in Abraham's day, as it had long before, and has ever since, in all the regions of Syria, Palestine, Arabia, and Egypt, in which criminals and prisoners of war were sold,--in which parents sold their children. Abraham, then, it is plain, bought, of the sellers in this traffic, men-servants and maid-servants; he had them born in his house; he received them as presents.

Do you tell me that Abraham, by divine authority, made these servants part of his family, social and religious? Very good. But still he regarded them as his slaves. He took Hagar as a wife, but he treated her as his slave,--yea, as Sarah's slave; and as such he gave her to be chastised, for misconduct, by her mistress. Yea, he never placed Ishmael, the son of the bondwoman, on a level with Isaac, the son of the freewoman. If, then, he so regarded Hagar and Ishmael, of course he never considered his other slaves on an equality with himself. True, had he been childless, he would have given his estate to Eliezer: but he would have given it to his slave. True, had Isaac not been born, he would have given his wealth to Ishmael; but he would nave given it to the son of his bondwoman. Sir, every Southern planter is not more truly a slave-holder than Abraham. And the Southern master, by divine authority, may, to-day, consider his slaves part of his social and religious family, just as Abraham did. His relation is just that of Abraham. He has slaves of an inferior type of mankind from Abraham's bondmen; and he therefore, for that reason, as well as from the fact that they are his slaves, holds them lower than himself. But, nevertheless, he is a slave-holder in no other sense than was Abraham. Did Abraham have his slave-household circumcised? Every Southern planter may have his slave-household baptized. I baptized, not long since, a slave-child,--the master and mistress offering it to God. What was done in the parlor might be done with divine approbation on every plantation.

So, then, Abraham lived in the midst of a system of slave-holding exactly the same in nature with that in the South,--a system ordained of God as really as the other forms of government round about him. He, then, with the divine blessing, made himself the master of slaves, men, women, and children, by buying them,--by receiving them in gifts,--by having them born in his house; and he controlled them as property, just as really as the Southern master in the present day. I ask now, _was Abraham a man-stealer?_ Oh, no, you reiterate: but the Southern master is. Why?

Is the Southern Master a Man-Stealer_?

Do you, sir, or anybody, contend that the Southern master seized his slave in Africa, and forcibly brought him away to America, contrary to law? That, and that alone, was and is kidnapping in divine and human statute. No. What then? Why, the abolitionist responds, The African man-stealer sold his victim to the slave-holder; he, to the planter; and the negro has been ever since in bondage: therefore the guilt of the man-stealer has cleaved to sellers, buyers, and inheritors, to this time, and will through all generations to come. That is the charge.

And it brings up the question so often and triumphantly asked by the abolitionist; _i.e._ "You," he says to the slave-holder,--"you admit it was wrong to steal the negro in Africa. Can the slave-holder, then, throw off wrong so long as he holds the slave at any time or anywhere thereafter?" I answer, yes; and my reply shall be short, yet conclusive. It is this:--_Guilt_, or criminality, is that state of a moral agent which results from his actual commission of a crime or offence knowing it to be crime or violation of law. That is the received definition of _guilt_, and _you_, I know, do accept it. The _guilt_, then, of kidnapping terminated with the man-stealer, the seller, the buyer, and holders, who, knowingly and intentionally, carried on the traffic contrary to the divine law. THAT GUILT attaches in no sense whatever, as a personal, moral responsibility, to the present slave-holder. Observe, I am here discussing, _not the question of mere slave-holding,_ but whether the master, who has had nothing to do with the slave-trade, can now hold the slave without the moral guilt of the man-stealer? I have said that that guilt, in no sense whatever, rests upon him; for he neither stole the man, nor bought him from the kidnapper, nor had any complicity in the traffic. Here, I know, the abolitionist insists that the master is guilty of this _complicity_, unless he will at once emancipate the slave; because, so long as he holds him, he thereby, personally and _voluntarily, assumes the same relation which the original kidnapper or buyer held to the African_.

This is Dr. Cheever's argument in a recent popular sermon. He thinks it unanswerable; but it has no weight whatever. It is met perfectly by adding one word to his proposition. Thus:--The master does NOT _assume the same relation which the original man-stealer or buyer held to the African_. The master's relation to God and to his slave is now wholly changed from that of the man-stealer, and those engaged in the trade; and his obligation is wholly different. What is his relation? and what is his obligation? They are as follows:----

The master finds himself, with no taint of personal concern in the African trade, in a Christian community of white Anglo-Americans, holding control over his black fellow-man, who is so unlike himself in complexion, in form, in other peculiarities, and so unequal to himself in attributes of body and mind, that it is _impossible, in every sense_, to place him on a level with himself in the community. This is his relation to the negro. What, then, does God command him to do? Does God require him to send the negro back to his heathen home from whence he was stolen? That home no longer exists. But, if it did remain, does God command the master to send his Christianized slave into the horrors of his former African heathenism? No. God has placed the master under law entirely different from his command to the slave-trader.

God said to the trader, Let the negro alone. But he says to the present master, _Do unto the negro all the good you can; make him a civilized man; make him a Christian man; lift him up and give him all he has a right to claim in the good of the whole community_. This the master can do; this he must do, and then leave the result with the Almighty.

We reach the same conclusion by asking, What does God say to the negro-slave?

Does he tell him to ask to be sent back to heathen Africa? No. Does he give him authority to claim a created equality and unalienable right to be on a level with the white man in civil and social relations? No. To ask the first would be to ask a great evil; to claim the second is to demand a natural and moral impossibility. No. God tells him to seek none of these things. But he commands him to know the facts in his case as they are in the Bible, and have ever been, and ever will be in Providence:--that he is not the white man's equal,--that he can never have his level--that he must not claim it; but that he can have, and ought to have, and must have, all of good, in his condition as a slave, until God may reveal a higher happiness for him in some other relation than that he must ever have to the Anglo-American. The present slave-holder, then, by declining to emancipate his bondman, does not place himself in the guilt of the man-stealer or of those who had complicity with him; but he stands exactly in that NICK _of time and place_, in the course of Providence, where _wrong_, in the transmission of African slavery, _ends_, and right begins.

I have, sir, fairly stated this, your strongest argument, and fully met it. _The Southern master is not a man-stealer._ The abolitionist--repulsed in his charge that the slave-owner is a kidnapper, either in fact or by voluntarily assuming any of the relations of the traffic--then makes his impeachment on his second affirmation, mentioned at the opening of this letter. That the slave-holder is, nevertheless, thus _guilty_, because, in the simple fact of being a master, he steals from the negro his unalienable right to freedom.

This, sir, looks like a new view of the subject. The crime forbidden in the Bible was stealing and selling a man; _i.e._ seizing and forcibly carrying away, from country or State, a human being--man, woman, or child--contrary to law, and selling or holding the same. But the abolitionist gives us to understand this crime rests on the slave-holder in another sense:--namely, that he steals from the negro a metaphysical attribute,--his unalienable right to liberty!

This is a new sort of kidnapping. This is, I suppose, _stealing the man from himself_, as it is sometimes elegantly expressed,--robbing him of his body and his soul. Sir, I admit this is a strong figure of speech, a beautiful personification, a sonorous rhetorical flourish, which must make a deep impression on Dr. Cheever's people, Broadway, New York, and on your congregation, Washington Square, Philadelphia; but it is certainly not the Bible crime of man-stealing. And whether the Southern master is guilty of this sublimated thing will be understood by us when you prove that the negro, or anybody else, has such metaphysical right to be stolen,--such transcendental liberty not in subordination to the good of the whole people. In a word, sir, this refined expression is, after all, just the old averment that the slave-holder is guilty of _sin per se!_ That's it.

I have given you, in reply, the Old Testament. In my next, I propose to inquire what the New Testament says in the light of the Golden Rule.

F.A. Ross.

Huntsville, Ala., Jan. 31, 1857.

The Golden Rule.

This view of the Golden Rule is the only exposition of that great text which has ever been given in words sufficiently clear, and, with practical illustrations, to make the subject intelligible to every capacity. The explanation is the truth of God, and it settles forever the slavery question, so far as it rests on this precept of Jesus Christ.

No. IV.

Rev. Albert Barnes:--

Dear Sir:--The argument against slave-holding, founded on the Golden Rule, is the strongest which can be presented, and I admit that, if it cannot be perfectly met, the master must give the slave liberty and equality. But if it can be absolutely refuted, then the slave-holder in this regard may have a good conscience; and the abolitionist has nothing more to say. Here is the rule.

"Therefore, all things whatsoever ye would that men should do to you, do ye even so to them; for this is the law and the prophets." (Matt. vii. 12.)

In your "_Notes_," on this passage you thus write:--"This command has been usually called the Savior's _Golden Rule_; a name given to it on account of its great value.--All that you EXPECT or DESIRE _of others, in similar circumstances_, DO TO THEM."

This, sir, is your exposition of the Savior's rule of right. With all due respect, I decline your interpretation. You have missed the meaning by leaving out ONE word. Observe,--you do not say, All that you OUGHT to expect or _desire_, &c., THAT do to them. No. But you make the EXPECTATION or DESIRE, which every man ACTUALLY HAS _in similar circumstances_, THE MEASURE of his DUTY to every other man. Or, in different words, you make, without qualification or explanation, the MERE EXPECTATION or DESIRE which every man,--with no instruction, or any sort of training,--wise or simple, good or bad, heathen, Mohammedan, nominal Christian,--WOULD HAVE _in similar circumstances_, THE LAW OF OBLIGATION, always binding upon him TO DO THAT SAME THING _unto his neighbor!_

Sir, you have left out the very idea which contains the sense of that Scripture. It is this: Christ, in his rule, presupposes that the man to whom he gives it _knows_, and from the Bible, (or providence, or natural conscience, so far as in harmony with the Bible,) the various relations in which God has placed him; and the respective duties in those relations; _i.e._ The rule assumes that he KNOWS what he OUGHT to expect or desire in similar circumstances.

I will test this affirmation by several and varied illustrations. I will show how Christ, according to your exposition of his rule, speaks on the subject,--of _revenge, marriage, emancipation_,--the fugitive from bondage. And how he truly speaks on these subjects.

Revenge--Right according to your view of the Golden Rule_.

Indian and Missionary--Prisoner tied to a tree, stuck over with burning splinters.

Here is an Indian torturing his prisoner. The missionary approaches and beseeches him to regard the Golden Rule. "Humph!" utters the savage: "Golden Rule! what's that?" "Why" says the good man, "all that you expect or desired other Indians, in similar circumstances, do you even so to them." "Humph!" growls the warrior, with a fierce smile,--"Missionary--good: that's what I do now. If I was tied to that tree, I would expect and desire him to have his revenge,--to do to me as I do to him; and I would sing my death-song, as he sings his. Missionary, your rule is Indian rule,--good rule, missionary. Humph!" And he sticks more splinters into his victim, brandishes his tomahawk, and yells.

Sir, what has the missionary to say, after this perfect proof that you have mistaken the great law of right? Verily, he finds that the rule, with your explanation, tells the Indian to torture his prisoner. Verily, he finds that the wild man has the best of the argument. He finds he had left out the word OUGHT; and that he can't put it in, until he teaches the Indian things which as yet he don't know. Yea, he finds he gave the commandment too soon; for that he must begin back of that commandment, and teach the savage God's ordination of the relations in which he is to his fellow-men, before he can make him comprehend or apply the rule as Christ gives it.

Marriage--Void under your Interpretation of the Golden Rule.

Lucy Stone, and Moses--Lady on sofa, having just divorced herself--Moses, with the Tables of the Law, appears: she falls at his feet, and covers her face with her hands.

This woman, everybody knows, was married some time since, after a fashion; that is to say, protesting publicly against all laws of wedlock, and entering into the relation so long only as she, or her husband, might continue pleased therewith.

Very well. Then I, without insult to her or offense to my readers, suppose that about this time she has shown her unalienable right to liberty and equality by giving her husband a bill of divorcement. Free again, she reclines on her couch, and is reading the Tribune. It is mid-day. But there is a light, above the brightness of the sun, shining round about her. And _he_, who saw God on Sinai, stands before her, the glory on his face, and the tables of stone in his hands. The woman falls before him, veils her eyes with her trembling fingers, and cries out, "Moses, oh, I believed till now that thou practised deception, in claiming to be sent of God to Israel. But now, I know thou didst see God in the burning bush, and heard him speak that law from the holy mountain. Moses, I know ... I confess.".... And Moses answers, and says unto her, "Woman, thou art one of a great class in this land, who claim to be more just than God, more pure than their Maker, who have made their inward light their God. Woman, thou in '_convention_' hast uttered Declaration of Independence from man. And, verily, thou hast asserted this claim to equality and unalienable right, even now, by giving thy husband his bill of divorcement, in thy sense of the Golden Rule. Yea, verily, thou hast done unto him all that thou expectedst or desiredst of him, in similar circumstances. And now thou thinkest thyself free again. Woman, thou art a sinner. Verily, thine inward light, and declaration of independence, and Golden Rule, do well agree the one with the other. Verily, thou hast learned of Jefferson, and Channing, and

Barnes. But, woman, notwithstanding thou hast sat at the feet of these wise men, I, Moses, say thou art a sinner before the law, and the prophets, and the gospel. Woman, thy light is darkness; thy declaration of equality and right is vanity and folly; and thy Golden Rule is license to wickedness.

"Woman, hast thou ears? Hear: I, by authority of God, ordained that the man should rule over thee. I placed thee, and children, and men-servants, and maid-servants, under the same law of subjection to the government ordained of God in the family,--the state. I for a time sanctioned polygamy, and made it right. I, for the hardness of men's hearts, allowed them, and made it right, to give their wives a bill of divorcement. Woman, hear. Paul, having the same Spirit of God, confirms my word. He commands _wives_, and children, and servants, after this manner:--'Wives, submit yourselves unto your own husbands, as it is fit in the Lord; children, obey your parents in all things, for this is well pleasing unto the Lord; servants, obey in all things your masters according to the flesh; not with eye-service, as men-pleasers; but in singleness of heart, fearing God.' Woman, Paul makes that rule the same, and _that submission_, the same. The manner of the rule he varies with the relations. He requires it to be, in the love of the husband, even as Christ loved the church,--in the mildness of the father, not provoking the children to anger, lest they be discouraged,--in the justice and equity of the master, knowing that he also has a master in heaven: (Colossians.) Woman, hear. Paul says to thee, the man now shall have one wife, and he now shall not give her a bill of divorcement, save for crime. Woman, thou art not free from thy husband. Christ's Golden Rule must not be interpreted by thee as A. Barnes has rendered it; Christ assumes that thou believest God's truth,--that thou knowest the relation of husband and wife, and the obligations and rights of the same, _as in the Bible; then_, in the light of this _knowledge_, verily, thou art required to do what God says thou oughtest to do. Woman, thou art a sinner. Go, sin no more. Go, find thy husband; see to it that he takes thee back. Go, submit to him, and honor him, and obey him."

Emancipation--Ruin--Golden Rule, in your meaning, carried out

Island in the Tropics--Elegant houses falling to decay--Broad fields abandoned to the forest--Wharves grass-grown--Negroes relapsing into the savage state--A dark cloud over the island, through which the lightning glares, revealing, in red writing, these words:--"_Redeemed, regenerated, and disenthralled by the irresistible genius of universal emancipation"_.--[Gospel--according to Curran--and the British Parliament.]

Jamaica, sir, to say nothing of St. Domingo, is illustration of your theory of the Golden Rule, in negro emancipation. You tell the Southern master that all he would expect or _desire_, if he were a slave, he must do unto his bondman; that he must not pause to ask whether the relation of master and slave be ordained of God or not. No. You tell him, if he would expect or desire liberty were he a slave, that settles the question as to what he is to do! He must let his bondman go free. Yea, that is what you teach: because the moment you put in the word OUGHT, and say, all that you OUGHT to expect or _desire_,--_i.e._ all that you know God commands you to _expect_ or desire in your relations to men, _as established by him,_--THAT do to them. Sir, when you thus explain the Golden Rule, then your argument against slave-holding, so far as founded on this rule, is at once arrested; it is stopped short, in full career; it has to wait for reinforcement of FACT, which may never come up. For, suppose the FACT to be, that the relation of master and slave is one mode of the government ordained of God. Then, sir, the master, knowing that FACT, and knowing what the slave, _as a slave_, OUGHT to expect or _desire_, he, the master, then FULFILS THE GOLDEN RULE when he does that unto his slave which, in similar circumstances, he OUGHT to expect to be done unto himself. Now comes the question, OUGHT he then to expect or desire liberty and equality? THAT is the question of questions on this subject. And without hesitation I reply, The Golden Rule DECIDES that question YEA or NAY, absolutely and _perfectly_, as God's word or providence shows that the GOOD _of the family, the community, the state_, REQUIRES that the slave IS or IS NOT to be set free and made equal. THAT GOOD, _as God reveals it_, SETTLES THE QUESTION.

Let the master then see to it, how he hears God's word as to THAT GOOD.

Let him see to it, how he understands God's providence as to THAT GOOD. Let him see to it, that he makes no mistake as to THAT GOOD. For God will not hold him guiltless, if he will not hear what he tells him as to THAT GOOD. God will not justify him, if he has a bad conscience or blunders in his philosophy. God will punish him, if he fails to bless his land by letting the bond go free when, he OUGHT to emancipate. And God will punish him, if he brings a curse upon his country by freeing his slave when he OUGHT NOT to give him liberty.

So, then, _the Golden Rule does not_, OF ITSELF, reveal to man at all what are his RELATIONS _to his fellow-men; but it tells him what he is to_ DO, when he ALREADY KNOWS THEM.

So, then, you, sir, cannot be permitted to tell the world that this rule must emancipate all the negro slaves in the United States,--no matter how unprepared they may be,--no matter how degraded,--no matter how unlike and unequal to the white man by creation,--no matter if it be a natural and moral impossibility,--no matter: the Golden Rule must emancipate by authority of the first sentiments of the Declaration of Independence, and by obligation of the great law of liberty,--the intuitional consciousness of the eternal right!

No. The Rule, as said, presupposes that he who is required to obey it does already know the relations in which God has placed him, and the respective duties in those conditions. Has God, then, established the relations of husband and wife, parent and child, master and slave? Yes. Then the command comes. It says to the husband, To aid you in your known obligations to your wife,--to give you a lively sense of it,--suppose yourself to be the wife: whatsoever, therefore, you OUGHT, in that condition, to expect or _desire_, that, as husband, do unto your wife. It says to the parent, Imagine yourself the child; and whatsoever, as such, you OUGHT to expect or _desire, that_, as parent, do unto your child. It says to the master, Put yourself in the place of your slave; and whatsoever you OUGHT, in that condition, to expect or _desire, that_, as master, do unto your slave. Let husband, parent, master, know his obligations from God, and obey the Rule.

Fugitive Slave--Obeying the Golden Rule under your version_.

Honorable Joshua R. Giddings and the Angel of the Lord--Hon. Gentleman at table--Nine runaway negroes dining with him--The Angel, uninvited, comes in and disturbs the feast.

Giddings has boasted in Congress of having had nine fugitive slaves to break bread with him at one time. I choose, then, to imagine that, during the dinner, the angel who found Hagar by the fountain stands suddenly in the midst, and says to the negroes, "Ye slaves, whence came ye, and whither will ye go?" And they answer and say, "We flee from the face of our masters. This abolitionist told us to kill, and steal, and run away from bondage; and we have murdered and stolen and escaped. He, thou seest, welcomes us to liberty and equality. We expect and desire to be members of Congress, Governors of States, to marry among the great, and one of us to be President. Giddings, and all abolitionists, tell us that these honors belong to us equally as to white people, and will be given under the Golden Rule." And the angel of the Lord says to them, "Ye slaves, return unto your masters, and submit yourselves under their hands. I sent your fathers, and I send you, into bondage. I mean it unto good, and I will bring it to pass to save much people alive." Then, turning to the tempter, he says, "Thou, a statesman! thou, a reader of my word and providence! why hast thou not understood my speech to Hagar? I gave her, a slave, to Sarah. She fled from her mistress. I sent her back. Why hast thou not understood my word four thousand years ago,--that _the slave shall not flee from his master?_ Why hast thou also perverted my law in Deuteronomy, (xxiii. 15, 16?) I say therein, 'Thou shalt not deliver unto his master the servant which is escaped from his master unto thee: he shall dwell with thee, even among you, in that place which he shall choose, in one of thy gates where it liketh him best: thou shalt not oppress him.' Why hast thou not known that I meant the heathen slave who escaped from his _heathen master?_ I commanded, Israel, in such case, not to hold him in bondage. I made this specific law for this specific fact. Why hast thou taught that, in this commandment, I gave license to all men-servants and maid-servants in the whole land of Israel to run away from their masters? Why hast thou thus made me, in one saying, contradict and make void all my laws wherein I ordained that the Hebrews should be slave-owners over their brethren during years, and over the heathen forever? Why hast thou in all this changed my Golden Rule? I, in that rule, assume that men know from revelation and providence the relations in which I have placed them, and their duties therein. I then command them to do unto others what they thus know they ought to do unto them in these relations; and I make the obligation quick and powerful, by telling every man to imagine himself in such conditions, and then he will the better KNOW '_whatsoever_' he should do unto his neighbor. Why hast thou made void my law, by making me say, 'All that thou expectest or desirest of others, in similar circumstances, do to them'? I never imagined to give such license to folly and sin. Why hast thou imagined such license to iniquity? Verily, thou tempter, thou hast in thy Golden Rule made these slaves thieves and murderers, and art now eating with them the bread of sin and death.

"Why hast thou tortured my speech wherein I say that I have made of one blood all nations of men, to mean that I have created all men equal and endowed them with rights unalienable save in their consent? I never said that thing! I said that I made all men to descend from _one parentage!_ That is what I say in that place! Why hast thou tortured that plain truth? Thou mightest as well teach that all 'the moving creatures that have life, and fowl that fly above the earth, in the open firmament of heaven,' are _created equal_, because I said I brought them forth of the water. Thou mightest as well say that 'all cattle, and creeping thing and beast of the earth, _are created equal_, because I said I brought them forth _of the earth_, as to affirm the equality of men because I say they are of one blood. Nay, I have made men unequal as the leaves of the trees, the sands of the sea, the stars of heaven. I have made them so, in harmony with the infinite variety and inequality in every thing in my creation. And I have made them unequal in my mercy. Had I made all men equal in attributes of body and mind, then unfallen man would never have realized the varied glories of his destiny. And had I given fallen man equality of nature and unalienable rights, then I had made the earth an Aceldama and Valley of Gehenna. For what would be the strife in all the earth among men equal in body and mind, equal in power, equal in depravity, equal in will, each one maintaining rights unalienable? When would the war end? Who would be the victors where all are giants? Who would sue for peace where none will submit? What would be _human social life?_ Who would be the weak, the loving? Who would seek or need forbearance, compassion, self-denying benevolence? Who would be the grateful? Who would be the humble, the meek? What would be human virtue, what human vice, what human joy or sorrow? Nay, I have made men unequal and given them _alienable rights_, that I might INSTITUTE HUMAN GOVERNMENT and reveal HUMAN CHARACTER.

"Why hast thou been willingly ignorant of these first principles of the oracles of God, which would have made thee truly a Christian philosopher and statesman?"

Fugitive Slave--Obeying the Golden Rule as Christ gave it

Rev. A. Barnes and the Apostle Paul--Minister of the gospel in his study--Fugitive slave, converted under his preaching, inquiring whether it is not his duty to return to his master--Paul appears and rebukes the minister for wresting his Gospel.

With all respect and affection for you, sir, I imagine a slave, having run away from his master and become a Christian under your preaching, might, with the Bible in his hands and the Holy Spirit in his heart, have, despite your training, question of conscience, whether he did right to leave his master, and ought not to go back. And I think how Paul would listen, and what he would say, to your interpretation of his Epistle to Philemon. I think he would say,--

"I withstand thee to thy face, because thou art to be blamed. Why hast thou written, in thy '_Notes_,' that the word I apply to Onesimus may mean, not _slave_, but _hired servant?_ Why hast thou said this in unsupported assertion? Why hast thou given no respect to Robinson, and all thy wise men, who agree that the word wherein I express Onesimus's relation to Philemon never means a hired servant, but a _slave_,--the property of his master,--a living possession?

"Why hast thou called in question the fact that Philemon was a slave-holder? Why hast thou taught that, if he was a slave-holder when he became a Christian, he could not _continue, consistently_, to be a slave-owner and a Christian,--that if he did so _continue_, he would not be in _good standing_, but an offender in the church? (See Notes.)

"I say Philemon was the master of Onesimus, in the real sense of a slave-owner, under Roman law, in which he had the right of life and death over him,--being thereby a master in possession of power unknown in the United States. And yet I call Philemon 'our dearly beloved and fellow-laborer,' I tell him that I send to him again Onesimus, who had been unprofitable to him in time past; but now, being a Christian, he would be profitable. I tell him, I send him again, not a slave, (only,) but above a slave, a Christian brother, beloved, specially to me, but how much more unto him, both in the flesh and in the Lord. Dost thou know, Albert Barnes, what I mean by that word, _in the flesh?_ Verily, I knew the things wherein the master and the slave are beloved, the one of the other, in the best affections of human nature, and in the Lord! therefore I say to Philemon that he, _as master_, could receive Onesimus _as his slave_, and yet as a _brother_, MORE _beloved_, by reason of his relation to him as master_, than I could regard him! Yea, verily,--and I say to thee, Albert Barnes, thou hast never been in the South, and thou dost not understand, and canst not understand, the force, or even the meaning, of my words _in the flesh_; i.e. in the love of the master and the slave to one another. But Philemon I knew would feel its power, and so I made that appeal to him.

"Why hast thou said, that I did not send Onesimus back _by authority?_ I did send him back by authority,--yea, by authority of the Lord Jesus Christ? For it was my duty to send him again to Philemon, whether he had been willing to go or not; and it was his duty to go. But he was willing. So we both felt our obligations; and, when I commanded, he cheerfully obeyed. What else was my duty and his? Had I not said, in line upon line and in precept upon precept, 'Servants, obey in all things your masters according to the flesh; not with eye-service, as men-pleasers, but in singleness of heart, pleasing God'? (Coloss. iii. 22.) Had not Peter written, 'Servants, be subject to your masters with all fear; not only to the good and gentle, but also to the froward'? (1 Pet. ii. 18.) Onesimus had broken these commandments when he fled from his master. Was it not then of my responsibility to send him again to Philemon? And was it not Christ's law to him to return and submit himself under his master's hand?

"Why, then, hast thou not understood my speech? Has it been even because thou couldst not hear my word? What else has hindered? What more could I have said, than (in 1 Tim. vi. 1-5) I do say, to rebuke all abolitionists? Yea, I describe them--I show their principles--as fully as if I had called them by name in Boston, in New York, in Philadelphia, and said they would live in 1857.

"And yet thou hast, in thy commentary on my letter to Timothy, utterly distorted, maimed, and falsified my meaning. Thou hast mingled truth and untruth so together as to make me say what was not and is not in my mind. For thou teachest the slave, while professing not so to teach him, that I tell him that he is not to count his master worthy of all honor; that he is to despise him; that he is not to do him service as to a Christian faithful and beloved. No. But thou teachest the slave, in my name, to regard his Christian master an offender in the sight of Christ, if he continues a slave-owner.

"Thou tellest him to obey only in the sense in which he is to submit to injustice, oppression, and cruelty; and that he is ever to seek to throw off the yoke in his created equality and unalienable right to liberty. (See Notes.)

"This is what thou hast taught as my gospel. But I commanded thee to teach and exhort just the contrary. I commanded thee to say after this way:--'Let as many servants as are under the yoke, count their own masters worthy of all honor, that the name of God and his doctrine be not blasphemed. And they that have believing masters, let them not despise them, because they are brethren; but rather do them service, because they are faithful and beloved, partakers of the benefit. These things teach and exhort.'

"Thou, in thy 'Notes,' art compelled, though most unwillingly, to confess that I do mean slaves in this place, in the full and proper sense; yea, slaves under the Roman law. Good. Then do I here tell slaves to count their masters, even when not Christians, worthy of all honor; and, when Christians, to regard them as faithful and beloved, and not to despise them, and to do them service? Yet, after all this, do I say to these same slaves that they have a created equality and unalienable right to liberty, under which, whenever they think fit, I command them to dishonor their masters, despise them, and run away! Sir, I did never so instruct slaves; nay, I did never command thee so to teach them. But I did and do exhort thee not so to train them; for I said then and say now to thee, 'If any man teach [slaves] otherwise, [than to honor their masters as faithful and beloved, and to do them service,] and consent not to wholesome words, even the words of the Lord Jesus Christ, and to the doctrine which is according to godliness, he is proud, knowing nothing, but doting about questions and strifes of words, whereof cometh envy, strife, railings, evil surmisings, perverse disputings of men of corrupt minds, and DESTITUTE OF THE TRUTH, supposing that gain is godliness; from such withdraw thyself,'

"What more could I have said to the abolitionists of my day? What more can I say to them in this day? That which was true of them two thousand years ago, is true now. I rebuked abolitionists then, and I rebuke them now. I tell them the things in their hearts,--the things on their tongues,--the things in their hands,--are contrary to wholesome words, even the words of the Lord Jesus Christ. Canst thou hear my words in this place without feeling how faithfully I have given the head, and the heart, and the words, and the doings of the men, from whom thou hast not withdrawn thyself?

"Verily, thou canst not hear my speech, and therefore thou canst not interpret my gospel. Thou believest it is impossible that I sanction slavery! Hence it is impossible for thee to understand my words: for I do sanction slavery. How? Thus:--

"I found slavery in Asia, in Greece, in Rome. I saw it to be one mode of the government ordained of God. I regarded it, in most conditions of fallen mankind, necessarily and irresistibly part of such government, and therefore as natural, as wise, as good, in such conditions, as the other ways men are ruled in the state or the family.

"I took up slavery, then, as such ordained government,--wise, good, yea best, in certain circumstances, until, in the elevating spirit and power of my gospel, the slave is made fit for the liberty and equality of his master, if he can be so lifted up. Hence I make the RULE of magistrate, subject, master and servant, parent and child, husband and wife, THE SAME RULE; _i.e._ I make it THE SAME RIGHT in the superior to control the obedience and the service of the _inferior_, bound to obey, whatever the difference in the relations and service to be rendered. Yea, I give exactly the same command to all in these relations; and thus, in all my words, I make it plainly to be understood that I regard slavery to be as righteous a mode of government as that of magistrate and subject, parent and child, husband and wife, during the circumstances and times in which God is pleased to have it continue. I saw all the injustice, the oppression, the cruelty, masters might be guilty of, and were and are now guilty of; but I saw no more injustice, oppression, and cruelty, in the relation of master and slave, than I saw in all other forms of rule,--even in that of husband and wife, parent and child. In my gospel I condemn wrong in all these states of life, while I fully sanction and sustain the relations themselves. I tell the magistrate, husband, father, master, how to rule; I tell the subject, wife, child, servant, how to submit. Hence, I command the slave not to flee from bondage, just as I require the subject, the wife, the child, not to resist or flee from obedience. I warn the slave, if he leaves his master he has sinned, and must return; and I make it the duty of all men to see to it, that he shall go back. Hence, I myself did what I command others to do: I sent Onesimus back to his master.

"Thus I sanction slavery everywhere in the New Testament. But it is impossible for thee, with thy principles,--thy law of reason,--thy law of created equality and unalienable right,--thy elevation of the Declaration of Independence above the ordinance of God,--to sustain slavery. Nay, it is impossible for thee, with thy interpretation of Christ's Golden Rule, to recognise the system of servile labor; nay, it is impossible for thee to tell this slave to return to his master as I sent Onesimus back; nay, thou art guarded by thy Golden Rule. Thou tellest him that, if thou hadst been in his place, thou wouldst have _expected, desired_ freedom, that thou wouldst have run away, and that thou wouldst not now return; that thou wouldst have regarded thy created equality and unalienable right as thy supreme law, and have disregarded and scorned all other obligations as pretended revelation from God. Therefore thou now doest unto him '_whatsoever_' thou wouldst expect or desire him to do unto thee in similar circumstances; _i.e._ thou tellest him he did right to run away, and will do right not to return! This is thy Golden Rule. But I did not instruct thee so to learn Christ. Nay, this slave knows thou hast not not given him the mind of Christ; nay, he knows that Christ commands thee to send him to his master again. And thus do what thou OUGHTEST to expect or desire in similar circumstances; yea, do now _thy duty_, and this slave, like Onesimus, will bless thee for giving him a good conscience whenever he will return to his obedience. Thus Paul, the aged, speaks to thee."

So, then, the Golden Rule is the whole Bible; yea, Christ says it is-"the law and the prophets;" yea, it is the Old Testament and the New condensed; and with ever-increasing glory of Providence in one sublime aphorism, which can be understood and obeyed only by those who know what the Bible, or Providence, reveals as to man's varied conditions and his obligations therein.

I think, sir, I have refuted your interpretation of the Golden Rule, and have given its true meaning.

The slave-holder, then, may have a good conscience under this commandment. Let him so exercise himself as to have a conscience void of offence towards God and towards men.

Yours, &c. F.A. Ross.

Conclusion.

I intended to, and may yet, in a subsequent edition, write two more letters to A. Barnes. The _one_, to show how infidelity has been passing off from the South to the North,--especially since the Christian death of Jackson; the other, to meet Mr. Barnes's argument founded on the spirit of the age.

The End.

Printed in Great Britain
by Amazon